MW01228404

Locked Up Inside

The Mind of a Convict

Dr. Maria A. Jones

Copyright © 2023

Dr. Maria A. Jones

All Rights Reserved

ISBN: 979-8-89075-177-5

Contents

About the Author 7

Acknowledgments... 8

Foreword 10

Introduction... 11

Decision-Making by Criminals............................. 13

White Collar Criminal Profile.............................. 23

Chapter 1 25

    Understanding Crime 25

    The Criminal Mind: A Case Study 27

    All in The Mind 37

    Characteristics of the Criminal 48

    Incredible Facts about the Criminal Brain 63

Chapter 2... 71

    Nature v/s Nurture: Are Criminals Born or Made? 71

Chapter 3... 82

    What Makes a Criminal a Criminal?............. 82

Chapter 4... 87

    What Causes Criminal Behavior 87

    Individual Engagement in Criminal Activity............... 87

    Theoretical Explanations 88

    Prevent and Discourage Criminal Behavior 90

Chapter 5... 97

    Insight into Criminal Behavior..................... 97

Chapter 6 106

Rehabilitating Our Criminals 106

The Main Goal of the Prison System 122

Return to Society from Prison 133

Reentry 136

Challenges to Reentry 136

Effective Reentry Programs 137

Rehabilitation 140

Sentencing Policies of Rehabilitation 140

The System is Broken 141

Cognitive Behavior Treatment 150

The Development of a Criminal Mind 159

About the Author

Maria Jones is a respected leader in the substance use disorder/Harm Reduction field with a career spanning over 25 years. As Co-Owner of LIFE community Center Inc. and through her involvement with organizations like House of Metamorphosis, McAlister Institute, Phoenix House Foundation, Stepping Higher, and Total Deliverance Worship Center, she has made significant contributions. Maria has received Women of Valor Star awards and Manager of the Year recognition for her work. She holds degrees in Child Development, Christian Counseling, and Christian Psychology, as well as a PhD in Behavioral Science. Currently a professor at ACTS University, Maria has dedicated herself to helping others succeed and making a positive impact. She is the CEO of LIFE Recovery Services LLC, where she focuses on providing support services for individuals re-entering society and improving the lives of those affected by the criminal justice system and homelessness.

Acknowledgments

First, I give glory and honor to my Lord and Savior, Jesus Christ, who continues to lead me daily and has provided me with several changes in my life to be all that He needs of me. I would want to thank Buddy Hauser for starting a ministry called 'Jamming for Jesus,' which rescued my life, believed in me, and demonstrated God's power through love and kindness.

This book is dedicated to my children Richard, Devon, Daunte, Danesia, and my lovely grandchildren for their love, support, and understanding. Thank you for always believing in me and providing me with the fortitude and bravery to believe in myself. My son Darion, you are always in my heart, and you will never be forgotten, RIP.

To my dear husband, it is because of your life change from the bondage of self-destruction that I am inspired to let the world know that there is hope for the convict that still suffers. I love you all. Peace and blessings.

I would also like to thank Shavonne Williams for the push that she gave me to move forward. You are truly an inspiration in my life, I love you dearly, and thank you for being such an amazing person.

Last, but certainly not least, I would like to extend my gratitude to my beautiful Queen Elect Lady Rachelle Benson for being the person that she has been in my life and the best spiritual mom ever. You are a gem and I thank for your love, endless support and for always seeing the good in me.

Foreword

Locked Up Inside the Mind of a Convict is a revealing work of research that explores how criminal minds think, feel, and process external experiences. The title grabs you, and the content opens the door to revelation.

As the Vice President of the American College Theological Seminary International University of San Diego, I am elated to foreword this dynamic work. I have known Dr. Maria Jones for several years. She is observant, philosophical, and a phenomenal woman. She has the ability to dissect psychological theories in an abstract and interesting way.

Within each chapter, Dr. Maria Jones will take you on a journey inside the mind of a criminal. This incredible author will cause you to rethink what you thought you knew about the criminal mind. This book is insightful and thought-provoking. This work will educate you in numerous areas and should be added to your resource library.

Dr. Rachelle Benson

Vice President / American College Theological Seminary International University of San Diego.

Introduction

Are the brains of people who commit crimes distinct from those who do not commit crimes? This is a topic that interests me since I have seen that the thought process of a criminal seems to be rather distinct from the way in which other individuals receive information. The ways in which a criminal thinks and acts may have been learned and then reinforced by the individual's upbringing or the environment in which they were raised.

At the moment, it seems as if the major purpose of prisons is to take in criminals who have committed crimes, place them in timeout, and then let them out to do the same crime again. Nevertheless, it seems that prisons only promote illegal activity, discrimination, racism, and membership in gangs, even though they are supposed to be places where individuals may be rehabilitated. Because of this, many good people who might make a huge change in their life after being released from prison end up becoming disruptive and committing further crimes after they are released.

This book aims to explore whether new phenomena, contexts, and processes, such as a new form of abuse, or new effects on personality, an application of either new theory or governmental policy can expand the possibilities for criminological engagement. It also should focus on the general population as I would like to examine the different aspects of the findings.

We are no longer able to function with the current criminal justice system, and with things as they are, there is just an excessively huge population for the jail to only have one available choice, criminals who are capable of altering their behavior.

Bearing in mind the adverse effects of a prolonged prison sentence, we need to build a prison system to operate and deal with convicts who can't or won't re-adjust to life outside of jail. Prisons need to be rethought as rehabilitation institutions to assist prisoners who will alter their ways and become productive members of society.

This book investigates the causes of disparities in incarcerated people, primarily focusing on the cause and effect of "being locked up" with a mental illness and substance abuse. It will also assess people who engage in criminal behavior and how they are defined as "a population not fit to live in society."

Decision-Making by Criminals

Whether criminal decision-making is, a rational process is a heated topic of discussion when one asserts that crime is the role of choice. Before the classical school of criminology, crime was thought to be the product of the paranormal occurrence of demons, witches, ghouls, and other creatures. The preclassical era of criminology is separated into two periods: the preclassical and postclassical periods. Before the time of state intervention into private matters, each individual dealt with violations of their rights. This was a problem because of the continuous cycle of violence being perpetrated. Soon the State (and even the Church) took on dispensing law and order to the masses of the Middle Ages. This led to the Holy Inquisition period, which lasted from the twelfth century to the eighteenth century. During the Holy Inquisition, harsh and inconsistent punishment was the norm. Also, there was no protection against bogus allegations, meaning the burden of proof was on the accused to prove their innocence.

The classical school of criminology was a response to the harsh times of the Holy Inquisition. A product of the Enlightenment, it sought to replace the concepts of divine privileges for royalty and clergy with logic, intellectualism, and a humanitarian approach. The two chief ambassadors of the classical school of criminology are Cesare Beccaria (1738-1794) and Jeremy Bentham (1748-1832). Beccaria is widely recognized as the father of the classical school of criminology. In his essay Dei deliti e delle pene (On Crimes and Punishment), Beccaria asserted that humans are rational, have free will, and are hedonistic. He also claimed that clear warnings of punishments could prevent crime. To prevent crime, certainty, severity, and celerity of punishment must be present. Jeremy Bentham embraced the practical philosophy of replacing harsh and capricious punishments with humane punishments and protection against bogus allegations.

The classical school of criminology was the foundation of the modern criminal justice system in the Western world. Criminal law and criminal procedure now assume that people are rational actors, thanks to the classical school of criminology. In addition, penalties for crime became more humane, and policing turned into a deterrence base. Sir Robert Peel was responsible for the passage of the London Metropolitan Police Act in 1829, which organized the first modern police department based on the principles of deterrence.

Whether one believes in the deterrence theory depends on their ideology. Until the 1970s, the criminological community rejected the theory while being accepted by criminal justice practitioners. Both points of view are concurrently right and wrong. The tiger prevention fallacy is a humorous analogy drawn to illustrate the widespread fallacy that the absence of crime demonstrates the effectiveness of deterrence efforts. The story identifies a man snapping his fingers in the middle of New York City and claiming that his efforts have deterred tigers from congregating. The warden's survey is a humorous analogy drawn to illustrate the widespread fallacy that the presence of crime demonstrates that deterrence does not work. The story identifies a prison warden pointing to his inmates as proof of the absence of deterrence. Now there is care taken to distinguish between general deterrence, directed at the community in general, and specific deterrence, which is geared toward preventing a particular offender from committing an offense.

Tipping levels are the idea that punishment certainty, severity, and celerity must reach a minimum level before a deterrent effect can be reached. The total prevention of crime through threats of punishment is absolute deterrence; this is not possible. Marginal deterrence is possible. Marginal deterrence is the prevention of some, but not all, crime through threats of sanctions. Crime may not be prevented with marginal deterrence, but it may be shifted to other times, places, or forms. Most criminologists believe informal sanctions are more deterrent than the formal sanctions of the criminal justice system. For example, the shame of being exposed as a deviant to friends and family is more threatening than official sanctions. John Braithwaite asserted that shaming someone served to shape one's conscience.

The crimes that seem to be the most deferrable seem to be rational, instrumental, mala prohibit (acts that are not inherently evil but prohibited for other reasons), and typically committed in public places. Evidence of the detectability of drunk driving is limited. Although, the sanctions associated with drunk driving may have a moral education effect. Capital punishment as a deterrent has little effect partly because of the irrational nature of acts punishable by death. There is considerable support for a brutalization effect where it seems that violent crime tends to increase after an execution.

Some factors make someone more or less deterrable. Those who are future-oriented, have high self-control, are low risk-takers, have an authoritarian personality, are pessimistic, and are older. Also, those who are from higher classes are more deterrable. Females are more deterrable than males. Those who have much to lose and little to gain are also in this category. Surprisingly, race has very little to do with one's level of deterrence.

Cesare Beccaria contended that they had to be rational for someone to be deterred. Contemporary deterrence expands conventional deterrence by considering the choices made by potential offenders and the choices made by potential victims.

Lawrence Cohen and Marcus Felson came up with the routine activities theory to explain rising crime rates in the 1970s. The routine activities theory is a theory of victimization comprised of three variables that contribute to the likelihood of a crime being committed. The first of the three variables is the abundance of motivated offenders. Motivated offenders are those who commit crimes whenever viable opportunities are encountered. The presence of suitable targets is the second variable. A suitable target is something or someone of value available to a potential offender. The absence of capable guardians is the third variable. This is when neither persons nor other agents are present to protect the property or vulnerable persons. The rationale of this theory is that one's lifestyle may expose them to opportunities or experiences that increase their odds of being an offender or a victim.

The Application and Robustness of the Rational Choice Perspective in the study of Intoxicated and Angry Intentions to Aggress.

The hypothesis was that the rational choice model is robust across different states of mind. The model's explanatory power is comparable, and its structural integrity is maintained across participants in different experimental conditions.

The procedure from Exum is as follows: Those persons interested in participating in the study contacted the experimenter, who described the study as an examination of the effects of alcohol on cognitive skills, mood, and social behavior. The experimenter also explained the inclusion criteria for the study (e.g., participants must be of legal drinking age, must fast before the study, etc.) and screened individuals using the Brief MAST. Those who met all inclusion criteria were scheduled for an appointment to complete the study.

All participants completed the study individually. Each participant was greeted upon their arrival by a male research assistant; the experimenter (also male) was not present. The research assistant verified that the participant was of legal drinking age, recorded the participant's height and weight, provided the participant with a manila envelope to place all his completed questionnaires, and administered the Background Questionnaire and Time 1 Mood Questionnaire. As the participant completed this latter task, the research assistant excused himself to retrieve the experimenter. The experimenter's helper went outside after reviewing the randomization schedule to obtain some food and drink.

Upon meeting the participant, the experimenter introduced himself and positioned a financial ledger book on the table near the participant. Inside the book, but visible to the participant, were five five-dollar bills. The experimenter informed the participant that this money, which he would receive after the study, was his participation payment. After reviewing the study procedures and informing the participant of the beverage he would be asked to consume, the experimenter administered the Time 1 breath test, explained the video game task, and began preparing the participant's drinks as the participant practiced the video game. Once comfortable with the procedures, the participant was instructed to play the game again to determine his baseline.

The participant then consumed the prescribed beverage. The experimenter engaged the participant in various tasks during the absorption period to prevent participant boredom. For example, the experimenter administered the first Cognitive Task and the Time 2 Mood Questionnaire and then explained the instructions for each of the remaining tasks. The experimenter casually mentioned to the subject as he read through the Scenario Packet instructions that the participant may envision him as the character. Joe in the story if it helped to make the scenario more vivid. This interchange was designed so that the participant would ideally envision himself engaged in a potentially violent confrontation with the experimenter when reading the story. Next, the experimenter reminded the participant that he would be playing the video game again later in the study and that the participant could win an additional $25 based on his performance during this task.

At this point in the study, approximately 5 minutes would remain in the absorption period. Therefore, the experimenter instructed the participant to complete the second Cognitive Task and the Time 2 breath test. The participant was then told to sit for a brief (approximately two-minute) rest period. The anger manipulation occurred during this time.

For those assigned to the No-Anger condition, the experimenter casually looked at his watch, indicated he needed to check on another participant in a nearby room, and instructed the research assistant to? Finish up here? And then left the room. For those participants assigned to the Anger condition, the experimenter casually looked at his watch, appeared puzzled by the time, and asked the research assistant if his watch was correct. In response to the research assistant's affirmation of the correct time, the researcher whispered, but loud enough for the subject to hear. What's going on? Are we running behind?

Appearing confused by this? The experimenter

questioned what time the participant arrived at the lab. After the participant responded, the experimenter accused the participant of coming to the study 30 minutes late and conflicting with the next scheduled appointment. To make these accusations appear more unjust and more likely to instill anger, the experimenter argued that the participant had previously phoned to reschedule his appointment. The angered experimenter reacted forcefully when subjects complained that the experimenter was wrong and had not rescheduled. (Pilot testing revealed that challenging participants' honesty with such an emotionally charged word induced anger more effectively.)

The experimenter refused to hear any additional arguments and instructed the research assistant to finish up here while attempting to call and reschedule the next participant. After taking a few steps, the experimenter left the room and returned to the laboratory with an apparent afterthought. He then took the ledger book containing the money off the table, turned to the participant, and stated? I do not think we can pay you the total of twenty-five dollars for this and then leave the room again. With the experimenter out of the room and the 25-minute absorption period completed, the research assistant administered the Time 3 breath test and the Scenario Packet. The participant then completed the video game, the Time 4 breath test, and the Exit Questionnaire. During this latter task, the research assistant excused himself to retrieve the experimenter, who returned to debrief the participant on the true purpose of the study and the experimental manipulations. All participants were paid in full. Sober participants were excused immediately, whereas intoxicated participants were escorted to a nearby room to sober up before leaving.

The findings suggest no single rational choice model underlies the decision to engage in physical assault. Perceived costs and benefits do not carry the same relative weight across hot and cognitive states within the hedonic calculus. Those who were drunk and/or upset were less concerned about the costs and people's goals. The egoistic goals assumed under the self-interest standard exist and are essential. Yet there is compelling evidence that many people are willing to make significant financial sacrifices to pursue a variety of other less egoistic goals. The adaptive rationality standard provides a moral basis for expanding the repertoire of assumed goals. Although it is difficult to prove that a particular non-egoistic taste is adaptive on balance, it can often be shown that such a taste confers benefits and costs. If we also know that the taste is widespread, the burden of proof should rest on those who insist that it be excluded from the utility function.

White Collar Criminal Profile

A significant amount of research has been conducted to determine what makes a white-collar criminal. While I have thus far only mentioned the potential causes behind white-collar crimes in passing, I aim to look at these causes in a lot more detail in this section.

Researchers are hoping that a specific type of profile could be established to have the ability to catch white-collar criminals at the beginning stage of their illegal activity, such as fraud. By reading about recent white-collar criminal cases in the news, we can come to the unfortunate realization that most white-collar criminals do not get caught.

The Association of Certified Fraud Examiners (ACFE) has done significant research and has been at the forefront of studying white-collar crime. The sad part of the entire research shows that the ACFE's profile description of a white-collar criminal describes the white-collar criminal as law-abiding citizens. The ACFE describes their idea of a white-collar criminal as someone who is "young, well-educated, aggressive go-getters who [get] tripped up along the way."

Furthermore, the ACFE elaborates on the noticeable red flags of white-collar criminals and how these signs may aid law enforcement agencies in arresting these individuals. 43% of the cases involving white-collar criminals showed that they lived way beyond their means. In a 2008 article, it was revealed that white-collar criminals are typically men averaging between forty-one years to fifty years old and working in a company's accounting department. As discussed, profiles can be established; however, there are some discrepancies in a perfect profile describing a white-collar criminal.

Chapter 1

Understanding Crime

Some crimes happen daily, and you ask yourself, why? How could this happen? How could they do this? But anything could happen when you are locked up inside your head. In this chapter, I want to examine the psychological maltreatment of the criminal mind of convicted people.

Predominantly convicts are expected to express their abuse experience through aggressive behavior and slip to display antisocial behavior such as drug abuse. And this can further develop into a personality disorder that can reflect into a conduct disorder. An individual is arrested in the cycle of violence where abused individuals from somebody become abusers of someone else, and this aggressive behavior is the only response to similar experienced situations. However, a single predictor of crime will not guarantee offending behavior in the future but can only be considered when we want to assess the causation of criminal behavior.

Anti-social behavior is behavior that infringes the law and rules that negatively affect the social order and other people. Various forms of anti-social behavior can result in a range of victimization, such as psychological victimization – verbal abuse, physical victimization – rape or battering, common victimization – vandalism, and economic victimization – robbery. Raising children in a single-family in socially deprived areas and ways.

An anti-social person can have feelings of hostility, low self-esteem, or depression that can damage another person by inflicting an injury. When we want to assess the risk of crime, then we need to know about the background of criminals and the environment and what possibilities and opportunities might lead to crime.

This chapter will address multiple aspects of psychological abuse, for instance, PTSD - post-traumatic stress disorder, the offender's personality – aggressive or hyperactive behavior, physical and sexual maltreatment, bullying from relatives and friends in the living environment, impulsiveness, intimidation, and domestic violence. The main reason crime occurs in society perhaps lies in various negative aspects of life. Then it is followed by opportunities to improve living standards for those affected and gain access to services that helps in well-being because those services, such as dental care, are charged with a higher fee.

Those aspects are almost not removable in society, which is why the potentiality for crime is latent and later attracts more occasions than would relate to conformity with social rules. Hence, many scholars argue that living under psychological mistreatment during childhood will reflect a higher crime rate in people with antisocial personalities in later life. Interventions that can be made to prevent the crime rate of those individuals might be missing, which led them to be involved with criminal justice. According to the Ministry of Justice (2016), there are currently 85 636 incarcerated people in the country. Taking into account these large numbers, we must attempt to understand the workings of the criminal mind so that we may better address their needs and allow them to readjust to society.

The Criminal Mind: A Case Study

Before judging others, we must educate ourselves and learn about them. This statement encompasses several ideas about being locked up. It is time for society to listen to and comprehend the call for assistance. We no longer need to be worried about these people being locked up behind bars; instead, we should be concerned about them being locked up inside themselves.

Being psychologically imprisoned may be a very lonely place. When we look at men and women in jail, we only see their crimes. Because of their poor decisions in life, criminals are regarded and treated negatively by society. People don't realize how tough it is for criminals to remain valuable members of society and the daily war they face inside themselves. Why do people always presume that a guy with a tattoo comes from a prison? Why do we presume that someone who has committed a crime is dangerous? It is important for society to address these questions, along with the underlying biases that may be at play here.

Taking into consideration these spiking numbers, it is imperative that we ask ourselves the question: what is going through someone's mind when they are committing a crime? What triggers a person to commit a murder or violent crime? There are many theories on why criminals commit these heinous crimes. Behavioral analysis examines why people commit crimes, what triggers a violent reaction, and how to prevent or predict these crimes from happening in the future.

Behavioral analysts focus on certain key concepts to piece together a crime and figure out the criminal's motivation behind the crime. These concepts include behavioral science, criminal profiling, victimology, and criminology. Behavioral science aims to improve human behavior by gaining a more excellent knowledge of how people think. Criminal profiling, on the other hand, can incorporate criminology and victimology.

The concentration of a crime and/or criminal is referred to as criminology, while victimology is the examination of victims and their psychological effects. It is quite a frequent occurrence for criminals to once have been victims of the crimes that they commit. Piecing behavioral science, criminology, and victimology will allow the analysts to create a criminal profile. Profiling is a tool that investigates colorism to forebode and profile the unknown offender.

For example, a murder was committed. There was no camera or witness, so the analyst will try to find DNA or some clue to describe the unknown offender's physical and emotional characteristics. Now, the analyst has an idea of who the unknown criminal could be. When evaluating a complex crime, the following behavioral manifestations left at crime scenes are considered: modus operandi behavior, ritual behavior, crime scene signature, and undoing behavior. Each of these behaviors leaves behind a trail of evidence that points toward the criminal. These behaviors also signify the motive the criminal might have had behind the crime. Ritual behavior refers to the criminal's specific order of events or actions before committing the crime. For instance, a murderer had a specific way of torturing or abusing the victim before killing them, which is then a marker that appears in every murder that they commit. Frequently, but not always, a murderer will leave a signature at the crime scene. They can be thought of as possible clues that narrow down a list of possible suspects. Undoing behavior is a psychological disorder in which the criminal will hallucinate or believe in magical illusions to undo their violent crime.

There are several types of criminals, but first, let me explain the more common types of criminals, which are not limited to serial killers, mass murderers, spree killers, and psychopaths. A murderer of three or more victims over a period of thirty days is considered to be a serial killer. The time in between the murders is usually taken as a "cooling-off period." Four or more murders simultaneously committed without any "cool off period" is mass murder. With mass murder, the murders are typically carried out in a single location, such as the attack on the World Trade Center, on 11th September 2001. Although that was a terrorist attack because the killer had a political plan, it is also considered mass murder. The Boston Bombing, The Virginia Tech Shooting, The Sandy Hook Elementary Shooting, and The Columbine High School Shooting are a few examples of mass murder spree killers, which is a mix of serial and mass murders. These criminals kill an unlimited number of victims in multiple locations. Spree killers tend to have almost no "cool off period" between murders.

A murderer who suffers from obstinate mental disorders and has extremely violent behavior is considered a psychopath. Psychopaths cannot create a personal relationship; therefore, they have no emotional guilt after committing a serious crime. They have a trait their doctors call "moral depravity" or "moral insanity." Psychopaths tend to have no sense of ethics and don't care about human rights. For "normal people," it's human nature to care about others or at least others we know. Psychopaths, however, have brains with weak connections among the brain's emotional systems components. These disconnects are responsible for their inability to feel emotions deeply. As a result, they cannot recognize fear or empathize with fellow human beings. Fear plays a significant role in our emotional and ethical behavior. Since they cannot recognize fear, they have no honest emotion acting as a motivation for their crimes.

Several complexities and dilemmas arise when dealing with the crimes committed by psychopaths. One may wonder how a psychopath can be put on trial if they don't know they have done wrong. There are many issues and debates about whether criminals with psychotic mental disorders or defects should be accountable for their crimes. This debate is called the 'Competency Evaluations,' and each state has its laws on this. For the state of Indiana, before the final submission, if the court has reasonable grounds to think the defendant cannot understand the proceeding, the defendant must undergo evaluations by a psychiatrist endorsed by the Indiana state board of examiners of health service providers in psychology.

After the evaluations, the examining psychologist will state if the defendant is competent for the trial or not. If the defendant lacks competency in the trial, it will be paused or delayed, or the defendant will be ordered to the division of mental health and addiction. This division will provide competency restoration services. Depending on the offense's statute, the defendant will be serviced by a third party either at their home, least restrictive setting or at the Department of Corrections. If the defendant is found competent, the trial will continue.

Criminology and victimology have critical roles in examining why the criminal committed the crime. Taking a closer look at their child's life, traumatic events, drug/alcohol abuse, and psychological/emotional issues can have a crucial role in determining their behavior.

Victimology refers to the psychological effects of being a victim. Any negative experience or traumatic event that the criminal has encountered as a child could also be why the criminal recreates that experience with their victims. For example, if an adult raped a child, it is possible that the adult was raped as a child and cannot control his impulses.

Another example could be a woman who was sexually assaulted, dangerously reacts to unwanted advances, and murders the man who is making advances. Furthermore, drugs and alcohol lead to more severe crimes than abusing illegal drugs and overusing alcohol. Some drugs, mixed with alcohol, can make a criminal hallucinate and violently lose control of self. These criminals may have no recognition of even committing the crime. Crimes of passion are good examples of psychological or emotional crimes. Criminals most often kill their partner, or spouse, out of impetuous outrage and heartbreak when catching their partner having sexual intercourse with another person.

Many theories argue that criminals are the aftermath of being raised aggressively due to where they live(ed) or a combination of nature versus nurture and that it is impossible to single out either nature or nurture as the reason that somebody becomes a psychopath.

There are, of course, other reasons at work. For instance, a distrust of mental health providers is highly prevalent among African Americans. Also, the cultural norms (e.g., mistrust of Whites) of Black clients can influence their paranoid behaviors, which White clinicians may not fully appreciate or understand. Although significant socio-political, scientific, and policy advances and service deliveries have occurred in mental health care into the millennium, care for African Americans continues to be plagued by barriers that emanate from their precarious history.

The African American population has been profoundly affected by the oppression and slavery they experienced in the United States. As a result, cultural mistrust seems to be related to severely mentally ill African Americans' attitudes toward White mental health clinicians. Therefore, sensitivity to these cultural beliefs may be necessary to keep them in the proper context and not commit diagnostic or treatment errors.

According to the Centers for Disease Control and Prevention, mental health disorders are common in the United States. Each year, one in two Americans has a diagnosable mental illness, including 44 million adults and 13.7 million children. In 2009, an estimated 11 million adults aged 18 or older, approximately 4.8% of all adults in the U.S., reported severe mental illness in the past years. Needless to say, this is a dire problem.

Each ethnic sub-group (defined by a shared heritage, beliefs, rituals, and traditions) demonstrated that there is no such thing as a homogeneous racial or ethnic community, according to the Surgeon General's report on Culture, Race, and Ethnicity. Each racial or ethnic group contained the full range of variation on almost every social, psychological, and biological dimension presented.

With over 20 years of experience working with formerly incarcerated and convicted individuals with co-occurring disorders (mental illness and substance abuse), community workers develop a vast understanding of the vicious cycle they live in and the daily struggle of trying and wanting to get out. Behavioral analysts who study the thinking patterns of criminals attest that for some criminals-to-be, antisocial behavior such as manipulativeness, impulsive active, and irresponsibility is prevalent.

Research on the criminal justice population has found criminal thinking prevalent among persons with severe mental illness. Their thinking styles are like those of incarcerated persons without serious mental illnesses. For most of us, it is hard to comprehend the urge to harm someone else as it is still something special. We consider the consequences to the victim, their family, and ourselves. Many criminal brains work differently than the average human. Of course, some people turn to crime after a tough childhood, but some criminals, especially psychopaths and those with personality disorders have minds wired for a crime.

I used to criticize criminals and believe they just needed to get their act together. I thought they should know better, so why do they continue to do what they do, get caught, and want the public to feel sorry for them? I thought there was no explanation for how they behaved and the difficulty they regularly got themselves into. Today, I have a fresh perspective on these men and women and their life.

It may be heartbreaking to hear about their experiences and hardships. It can be upsetting when you watch someone indulging in silly behaviors that are usual and normal for them. This includes things like violence and drug usage, homelessness, prostitution, lying, and manipulating to get what they want. I have never understood why men and women cycle in and out of prisons or treatment programs. We witness all this conduct, yet many do not strive to understand or do not care. Today, I would like to share a little realization with you.

We all suffer from something, and regrettably, the world closes its eyes to its people's needs due to fear and ignorance. People who commit crimes have antisocial characteristics such as manipulativeness, impulsivity, and recklessness. According to research on criminal justice populations, criminal thinking is frequent among inmates. A criminal's mind operates so that possibility or assumption becomes an actuality and thought becomes a reality. If someone sells a criminal, he may take it to guarantee that whatever they choose to do it as good as done. The outcome is that if they approach a criminal action, the condition of perfect confidence is obtained. A criminal's manner of thinking is not a natural state of mind. Criminals prefer to think about things and occurrences rather than identifying criminal thinking patterns and rectify them. As I have attempted to illustrate in this section, however, the solution is rarely as straightforward as that. Nature and nurture act in an intertwined manner, and if we are to make rehabilitation and readjustment easier for criminals, we need to address both of these components.

All in The Mind

Many people wonder why some people are able to do bad things, even when they know the consequences. To our normal brains, there seems to be no reason for doing things like this.

To figure out who would be the most likely to commit criminal acts, criminals' brains must be analyzed to see if there are some early warning signs, such as inherited psychological disorders and traits. Studies have shown that some psychological disorders are passed down from parents to children. In adverse conditions, these psychological issues will develop in the child and may even manifest in a manner worse than they did in the parents. Depending on what these psychological disorders are, they can lead to violent or criminal acts if not monitored and aided early on.

In the same vein, another early warning of later problems is inherited character traits. Certain personality traits, such as aggression, difficulty managing anger, jealousy, and grudge-holding, can be inherited and passed down from one generation to the other. These traits can make certain individuals more likely to have violent tendencies if they are not controlled. There is no way to prevent these inherited factors, but with the right tactics, they can be controlled and managed.

The other factor in determining if someone is likely to perform criminal acts is the emergence of psychological problems that develop on their own accord. These problems can start to appear at any time in life, but most won't develop fully until the individual progresses to adulthood. Each one can cause problems in normal brain functioning and have adverse effects on the individual's personality.

Of these problems, perhaps the most dangerous is a condition called psychopathy, which is also sometimes referred to as 'moral insanity.'

As per the aforementioned definition, people suffering from psychopathy have no sense of morals or the ability to empathize with others. Everything else about them is normal, but they do not care for any other humans except themselves. Their psychopathy can cause them to perform violent actions against others and have no guilt of any kind.

Another problematic condition is called neurosis. This condition causes the mind to develop contradictions and defense mechanisms to justify the actions committed by the individual. A neurotic may be committing a criminal act, but with the utmost conviction that the move isn't ethically wrong. Any thought that enters the neurotic's mind will similarly comply with the brain's twisted logic.

Other psychological conditions that can attribute to criminal behavior include schizophrenia: which causes split personalities, and insanity. There is also delusion, which refers to a belief that your actions are correct and everything else in wrong. Moreover, there is paranoia, which refers to the act of believing that something must be done to save yourself or being irrationally scared of something, and several other diseases and conditions like these can also cause criminal behavior or violent action.

The causes of actual criminal behavior are varied. Most of the time, though, it is caused by the brain's belief that it can get some reward or it will help the person in some way. Humans want things to survive or to make them happy and will often take the fastest way of getting to them. The quickest way to get them is to steal. If there is no self-control, then stealing is a desirable choice.

The brain may also feel that a criminal act is justified if the action can solve some problem that the brain has. Humans also want to remain balanced with no problems. This sense of well-being is a survival tool that lets the brain know it is safe. If a problem arrives, some people will go to extreme lengths to remove the problem.

Often the brain can find some way to solve a problem without criminal action. However, if the brain sees no alternative ideas, it will. Sometimes there can seem to be no answer to a problem other than a violent or criminal act. Your brain makes it seem okay by making justifications for keeping you and yourself happy.

These previous decisions can make someone commit a criminal act, but others can also persuade them. People naturally urge to follow others who seem to be in charge. When a person in charge asks someone to do something, most people follow through, even if they disagree with the action. Being told to do something terrible by someone else helps your brain convince you that it is not your fault and is okay. Your brain believes the other person has all the blame, which removes any sense of guilt from your conscience.

The power of obedience can cause some of the most destructive acts. One strong example is terrorism. Most terrorist groups have some powerful ideal that helps and promote their cause. The people who follow this ideal become swept up in it. People desire an ideal to stand for that helps them deal with their lives. If taken too far, the ideal takes over their life, and they will do whatever the movement tells them to do. If people become too dedicated to an idea or organization, they can lose their sense of self and become an "agent of the cause." They will go to extreme lengths to help their cause in every way, even committing suicide.

Another extreme act that is caused by obedience to authority is genocide. The leading cause is if there is a high amount of nationalism or national pride, then people can start to believe that their nation is the greatest. As a consequence, this may generate a false sense of superiority over others. The nation and government will begin to find ways to justify their superiority. If a country lost a war or suffered a big disaster and started to have problems, they could try to find some scapegoat for their problems.

A genocide begins with simply disliking a particular race and then expands until the leader's will orders their extermination. A nation's leader can have negative feelings about a country or race and think they should be destroyed.

They can imprint this idea on others who follow them because of their authority. Stanley Milgram tested how far people would go to show obedience, even if the action was not something they agreed with,

"I observed a mature and initially poised businessman enter the laboratory smiling and confident. Within 20 minutes, he was reduced to a twitching, stuttering wreck...yet he [the participant] continued to respond to every word of the experimenter and obeyed it to the very end."

As this reveals, people will perform the actions they are told, even if every part of them wants them to stop.

Addiction is a severe problem for many people. It is incredibly difficult for people to stop, which creates lots of business for people who sell addictive substances. The sellers of dangerous drugs do not suffer from any of the hazardous effects of addiction. Many illegal drugs are also costly, and people who are addicted will pay the cost. The seller sells the drugs and does not suffer the dangerous effects or the dangerous behavior it can cause. All the harm is done to others, not them.

The actual cause of the addiction is a mix of three different factors. The first one is the pleasurable effects that most drugs have. The temporary effects of several dangerous drugs are quite pleasant to many people. They can cause your brain to become extra happy or have other effects that the brain likes.

The second and most potent factor is the brain's pleasure sensor. Often it is not the actual addiction to the drug that is the problem. It is the brain's want of the sensation of getting it. The brain releases a small amount of a chemical that makes you happy right before doing something you have become addicted to. The pleasure sensors in your brain want to be satisfied, and if they find something that does that, it is tough to stop it.

There is also a third part: the brain trying to cover up the negative effects so you will continue to have the addiction. The brain's desire for the substance it is addicted to can let it forget or overrule memories of the negative effects of the habit. The person will continue to be addicted, conscious of the adverse effects, but unable to help themselves.

Hate crimes, also known as violence against people of a particular group or race, have become a severe problem. The causes of these incidents are varied, but they can be narrowed down to three main reasons. The first one is because of a condition called xenophobia, which is a fear of people from other countries or races. An unnatural fear of people from another country can cause people to mistrust anyone from that country or race. It can also cause a violent and harmful reaction against them.

Another reason is that people blame others who are not like them for their trouble and seek some sort of justice. Blaming a particular group of people for problems in life can cause unnecessary negative feelings. Furthermore, this can develop further into violence against people of the other group.

People can also cause hate crimes by having prejudices against other people. Humans are more likely to stay or like people who resemble them and are similar in appearance. Sometimes people who look different are classified by the brain as a threat to its safety. When this happens, people will dislike and treat people of this group as inferior.

There are some problems with fighting against hate crimes. The most significant factor is that there have been no laws against violence because of someone's culture or race. This is because it is tough to identify specific cases. It is hard to identify because many are reluctant to say it happened. People's pride or fear can interfere with getting facts for instances of hate crimes. They do not want to say anything occurred because it may make them feel silly or weak.

Violent crimes are among the oldest and most dangerous forms of criminal behavior. The reasons that it happens are different for every case, but three main reasons are the most likely causes. The first one is someone who has over-aggressive behavior. People with more aggressive personalities and short tempers are likelier to exhibit violent tendencies. Sever anger stops blood flowing to the parts of your brain that control rational thinking, which may cause violent action without thinking.

Anger and resentment can be another cause if they create a negative feeling about a specific person. People like life to be fair, and if someone insults them or makes them mad, they want to get even. The brain will find ways to make things even; if violence seems the best way, it will typically follow. This phenomenon can lead to violence if the urge to get even is taken too far.

The third main reason is the ability to get away with the crimes and not have it traced to who did it. The brain will only perform extreme acts of violence if there is a high probability of no consequences. If the cost is too high, the brain will stop any action because it would seek too much of a risk.

It is often hard to predict or prevent violence because of several reasons. Many people suffer from a problem called the "passive bystander." This means that many people will not do anything if they see a problem because they would feel strange doing it alone. Most people are likelier to do something if they see someone do it first. They will assume that other people around them will do something to stop it.

Another big reason violence is difficult to prevent if someone sees it is that people are nervous about helping someone they do not know. If someone does not know the person well, their brain is much less likely to help. Their brain decided the perceived risk was much higher than the perceived benefit. They may also be worried about violence against themselves from the person attacking them.

Some people believe that criminal behavior is not caused by psychology. They are sure that some people are just "born bad." If someone's parents were criminals, then they would be criminals too. It is a part of their personality that they receive at birth. The urge to do criminal acts is stuck in their brain and cannot be removed. It cannot be fixed by therapy or other psychological means.

These people also believe that criminals are to be considered beyond help. If they did something wrong once, they would probably do it again. They can't stop themselves from acting like criminals. Since they cannot be changed, criminals must always be contained. The only answer is to keep them locked up so they can't do anything else.

This approach to criminal behavior is incorrect. There have been many cases of criminals being rehabilitated using psychological therapies. One of the best methods is the use of psychoanalysis. This psychological study of a person's mind can help doctors tell what sort of problems a criminal may have. Doing this can help fix their problems by identifying the best treatment for them.

Another good technique that doctors use to help criminals is counseling. This is when doctors listen to criminals tell them about their troubles. Assisting criminals to talk about what caused their actions helps them see what it's wrong and allows them to be able to fix it. If someone's brain realizes a problem, it will automatically try to start fixing the trouble.

These solutions work for most people, but some cases need extra help. Several medicines have been developed to help people with more serious psychological issues. Criminals with these conditions could take these medications to help stabilize their brains and help them work through the trouble. For severe illnesses like psychotic tendencies, criminals may be taken to notarized and official mental institutions. They can be cared for and helped to find cures for their conditions.

In conclusion, your brain is the creator of all your actions. When there is something wrong in the brain, your way of thinking and acting is shifted. This can cause violent and criminal behavior to form and occur. If we can help people who have these sorts of troubles, then we can bring about a great change for everyone.

Characteristics of the Criminal

In understanding how the criminal mind works and operates, we must comprehend the key characteristics of the criminal's mind to rehabilitate them more efficiently. Moreover, we must recognize the errors in our thinking patterns regarding criminals and seek to rectify them. With that said, the characteristics of the criminal's mind consist of the following:

Energy- Criminals are extremely energetic; their high level of mental activity is directed to a flow of ideas as to what would make life more interesting and exciting.

Fear — In criminals, fears are widespread, persistent, and intense. One of the most prevalent fears include the fear of being caught for something— either an injury or the murder of someone.

Zero State — Zero State refers to the experience of oneself as being nothing, a zero, a feeling of absolute worthlessness, hopelessness, and futility. Unfortunately, this is an experience that most criminals find themselves in.

Anger — Anger is a fundamental part of the criminal's way of life. They respond angrily to anything interrupted as opposing what they want. Anger is, for the criminal and is a significant way of controlling people and situations.

The Power Thrust — Criminals need control and power over others, which manifests in all areas of their lives. The most significant form of this power and excitement comes from committing a forbidden act and getting away with it. The occasions when criminals appear to show an interest in a responsible activity are generally opportunities for criminals to exercise power and control.

Sentimentality - Criminals are often excessively sentimental about their mothers, invalids, animals, babies, love attachments, and plans for the future.

Religion- Criminals use religion to support their way of thinking and criminality. Their religious ideas are usually very literal and concrete. Religion (like sentimentality) does not consistently deter criminal thinking or actions but does support the criminal's self-image as a good and decent person.

Concrete Thinking — Criminals tend to think about objects and events in a literal manner, and display a limited ability to deal with general and abstract concepts.

Fragmentation — Fragmentation is a fundamental feature of the criminal personality. It refers to radical fluctuations in the criminal's mental state within relatively short periods. A pattern of starting a project and then changing one's mind emerges. Criminals will make commitments that set sincerity and great feelings and then break these commitments within the hour. They may feel sentimental love for their children and then take their money to buy drugs. Isolated and contradicting fragments, hastily joined together, make up their characters. Being one of a kind highlights how distinct they are from everyone else. Moreover, criminals believe with the utmost conviction that they are different from everyone else.

Perfectionism — Criminals have high standards of perfection, and they apply them to their lives robotically and inconsistently.

Suggestibility — Criminals are incredibly susceptible to recommendations that lead to their desired outcomes. They tend to oppose any nudges toward more ethical thinking and action.

The Loner — Criminals lead a private, secretive life, one against the world, including fellow criminals. They feel apart from others, even if they are active and gregarious.

Sexuality — Criminals have plenty of sexual experience but little in the way of sensual gratification of competence and performance. They treat their sexual relationships as conquests and regard their partners as possessions.

Lying — For criminals, lying is a way of life. Lying is incorporated into their basic makeup and fuels other criminal patterns. More common than the premeditated lion, the criminal's habitual lying becomes automatic. The criminal defines reality with their lies and maintains and exerts control.

The Closed Channel — In treatment, open-channel communication requires disclosure, perceptive readiness, and self-criticism. Instead, the entire criminal case is secretive, has a closed mind, and is self-righteous. If therapy for the criminal is to be effective, an open channel between the criminal and their therapist ought to be established.

At the same time, criminals believe there is nothing they cannot do if they want to. Criminals say they can escape accountability for what they do. 'I' cannot also be translated to 'our.'

Ownership — When criminals want something that belongs to someone else, it is as good as theirs. Belonging exists in their minds because they feel justified in getting their way.

Criminals consider themselves decent people with the right to do whatever suits their purpose. They view the world as the oyster and people as ponds or checkers, waiting to be dealt with as they wish. They think it is chronic and without malice.

Fear of Fear — Criminals are fearful of fear and detest that emotion. When they serve fear in others, they point out scorn and exploit it. When fear occurs in them, it is a put-down that wreaks havoc on their self-esteem. Denying fear, anxiety, and doubt in themselves, the criminal tends to exploit these emotions when they occur in others.

Lack of Trust — Although criminals do not trust others, they demand this trust. There are times when the trust of others is sincere, but this is only one of the many fragments of their personalities. It does not last.

Refusal to be Dependent — Criminals depend on others for some things in life. However, they do not see themselves this way. They fail to believe that a degree of independence is a necessary part of existence. To them, dependence is a weakness, and they would do without it.

Lack of Interest in Responsible Performance — Criminals are not interested in responsible tasks that don't offer immediate excitement. They find responsibility boring. The interest is short-lived when they become interested in the accountable project unless they feel the excitement of being a suspicious success.

Pretentiousness — Criminals do little to achieve but care about tremendously inflated ideas about their capacities. They often consider themselves to be the best of the best. Some are correct, and others are wrong about their delusions. Often, they regard themselves as more knowledgeable than prison staff and seize every opportunity to teach others.

Failure to Make an Effort to Endure Adversity — Criminals expend little effort, though they may expend tremendous energy to do what they want. They refuse to endure the adversity of responsible living.

Poor Decision-Making for Responsible Living — There is no sound reasoning consideration of costs, or options in critical personal decisions. Criminals are reluctant to ask about not attending activities because they view it as a put-down to reveal their ignorance. They do not want to hear if the facts contradict their pretensions and expectations.

The Victim Stance — When criminals are held accountable for their irresponsible actions, they blame others and portray themselves as victims. The world does not give them what they think is essential, so they view themselves as poorly treated and, thus, a victim.

Lack of time and perception — Criminals demand immediate possession and success even more than wanting what they want when they want it. They must be the best and have the best right now.

Failure to put oneself in another's position — Criminals demand every consideration and every break for themselves but stop to think about what other people think, feel, and expect

Failure to consider injury to others — Criminals leave extensive injuries to those around them. However, I do not view myself as injuring others when held accountable. They regard themselves as the injured party.

Failure to assume obligation — The Constable obligation is foreign to criminal thinking since obligations interfere with what they want to do. For criminals, obligations are viewed as a position of weakness. If pressed with obligations, they will respond with resentment and anger.

Core efficient and cut-off — Criminals may be deterred from connectivity by a sense of conscience and a sincere wish to change. And by sentimental religious or humanitarian feeling of criminality by the processes of the core region and cut off.

Core history is a mental process in which deterrence is slowly eliminated until the desire to commit a criminal act outweighs the determining factors. This is a criminal scheming in this process; a criminal's sentiments, ideas, and fears gradually give way to the desire for illegal and criminal activity.

Cut off— This refers to a mental process that eliminates interiors from consideration entirely and instantaneously. It is a cognitive process that produces fragmentation criminals radically move instantaneously from one mental state to another.

Building up the opinion of oneself as a good person — Criminals believe they are good and decent people. They reject the thought that one of the criminals performs sentimental acts toward others. It has the criminal view of oneself as good; the image of themselves as a good person gives them intern license for more crimes and refers to the reoccurrence of the zero state

Deferment — Criminals defer to put things off in three days, one that carries the idea of an ultimate crime. They have built a habit of deferring minor routine responsibilities and paying a bill by the letter following the tax return.

Super optimism — A criminal's mind works to accomplish its possibility or assumption and ideas in reality. When someone sells a criminal, maybe he regards it as a promise; anything they decide to do is good. The criminal uses cut-off to eliminate fear and doubt. The result is that they approach criminal activity. The state of absolute confidence reads super optimistic. There is no doubt in their mind if they decide to become responsible. They are incredibly confident about their success. The criminal will believe the change is already a cure when this decision is made.

Criminals use everyday words that only make sense to them.

When conversing with the criminal, their frames of reference are completely different; therefore, they are conversing in different languages. Criminals have a view of life radically different from people who are responsible; they use words differently from most people. Professionals working in corrections and law-enforcement scholars say that assertions you counter in daily conversation have a very different meaning spoken by criminals.

When a criminal says he trusts someone, that is not a compliment. He means that he has a person under his control. The person agrees to go along with him or, at the absolute least, has a nocturnal affair with one of their businesses. Or they may mean that they count on a person not to snitch or inform them. This is very different from what most people mean when they speak of relying on someone with integrity and the ability to provide help, support, or comfort.

A criminal may appear paranoid, and that he seems unduly suspicious and distrustful is a feature of a severe mental illness in which a person is irrationally suspicious. In other words, with no basis in reality, a criminal has been a reason for being extremely doubtful because they have betrayed others and engaged in irresponsible conduct if not legal.

People like we are looking to hold them accountable. There is no mental illness involved. Even the word police have a different meaning for criminal. Mostly we use the term to refer to law enforcement officers. Criminal uses the words to refer to a person who checks up on them and holds them accountable.

Here are some words that you may hear from the mouth of criminals. They vividly illustrate a criminal's thinking and how different their thought process is from those of a responsible person.

Why study history? It is all in the past (lack of what time perception)

Crime is like a screen, it is delicious. Take my crime away, and you take my world away,

(Excitement of a criminal life)

This empathy thing will send it for me (failure to put oneself in the place of others)

Cops are dumb. They are not going to tell me what to do. They want to make arrests. It gives them something to do. (Life is a one-way street)

People think that if I get in serious trouble. My causes will bother me. I think about it.

They say I need help. They are the ones who need help. If something happened, it happened. I've done many things. I do not worry about it. (Ability to set off considerations of conscious)

I can't think of one thing that wasn't my parent's fault. (Stance as a victim)

If you lock the door, a window goes into his house. (Blaming the victim)

I'm well endowed. I have stuck it into women like a murderer sticks a knife. (Rapist sense of power over his victim).

I am a real neat guy. I deserve a neat girl. (Since of entitlement)

If I was raping her, why did not she scream? (Lack of a concept of injury to others)

It feels good to inflict pain. (Lack of a concept of injury to others)

I hate bourdon pain. The bills it's mind-numbing (contempt for the responsible life)

I was born on the wrong date, at the wrong time, and under the wrong star (Stance of the victim)

If a responsible person converses with the criminal, their frame of reference is entirely different and therefore is as though they are conversing in different languages.

Because criminals have a view of life that is radically different from responsible people, they use words differently. For most people, words commonly encountered in daily conversation have a different meaning when spoken by criminals. The examples above use words to which the criminal imparts a distinctive meaning. It is the meaning very different from what a responsible person intends to convey using the exact words in their interactions with criminals. Responsible people tend to be aware of these physical issues.

When offenders are held accountable, they offer explanations and widely behave as they did unless they make a full confession. The after-the-fact statements are usually intended to gain sympathy and minimize culpability. They focus on people and circumstances outside themselves often. This statement sounds plausible even to seasoned justice and mental health professionals.

***

A criminal may have plenty of excuses for a crime, but the situation gets exacerbated when mental health professionals follow in the same vein. Kleptomania may exist in the minds of mental health professionals, but it is a concept that offers an excuse rather than an explanation. The so-called kleptomaniac is someone who steals frequently and becomes good at it. He surveys the situation before committing the crime. If he spots security devices or personnel, he exits the situation and doesn't steal. Taking this into account, we may ascertain that the criminal makes a series of choices about what to steal and calculates when conditions are optional.

For the common man and woman, the idea of a person who steals things he already owns or can easily afford may seem baffling. A mental health professional may think that a psychological disorder can explain stealing. Habitual BB appears to suffer from compulsion. He may seem to resort to stealing to feel better while coping with depression.

Two evaluations coincide when a criminal is interrogated or interviewed about his illegal conduct. The detective psychologist or interviewer is examining him, but he is doing what he has done all his life, namely prying out others to target any vulnerability. In an interrogative setting, the criminal counts on outsmarting his interrogator.

This desire to outsmart the investigator can be observed even in relatively inexperienced interviewees. A common occurrence is that when apprehended, shoplifters often say things like,

"Everybody does it,"

"The store will miss it"

"I'll have the ready by X day,"

These transparent excuses after the act have little bearing on the actual motivation to steal. Similarly, depression has little bearing on the compulsion to steal. Thousands of people are depressed but are not tended to steal.

Other than depression, poverty has been considered by many to be a call to steal. However, poverty is a problem that effects thousands, and most poor individuals do not give into the compulsion to steal like the kleptomaniac. Peer pressure is another factor frequently cited by youngsters as the reason for shoplifting. Peer pressure to shoplift does occur, but the question in this instance becomes, how does the youth choose his peers? Kids and adults gravitate to others who share their interests. The child who claims "all my pals are doing it" discloses a great deal about his social circle and thus his personality.

It is critical to understand the motivation for crimes in order to not be deceived by perpetrators when they are held accountable for their actions and are searching for a means to evade the situation. When a criminal is in a problem, it usually means that he is in a situation created by zoning responsibility, and he wishes for someone to remove the obstacle in his path as quickly as possible. He may claim he needs help just to have another person assist him in a criminal adventure so that implant the consequences on someone else.

Having no concept of loyalty, criminals seldom use the word. When they do, it refers to a person who will be an accomplice or do precisely what they want. Criminals have no concept of love. When a criminal speaks of love, they are often referring merely to sex.

Most people experience boredom as a kind of weariness. When a criminal complains the boredom, more often than not, these feelings are experienced alongside hate. For the criminal, boredom refers to a state in which he is deterred from doing what he finds exciting or forbidden. Suppose that a mature, responsible person comes from a new experience, an extraordinary performance, and finds reality pale in comparison. Life without crime is much like that for a criminal. For a criminal, excitement comes from pursuing a conquest, a means to exercise power and control other people.

***

A criminal may appear paranoid and may seem unduly suspicious, and distrustful. Paranoia can be a feature of severe mental illness and is often characterized by an irrational suspicion and distrust of others. In some criminals, paranoia might just be another means to evade accountability.

Oftentimes, law enforcement officers are referred to as and treated as criminals. Rather than misuse the word, we must exercise caution in our use of the term and apply it to actual perpetrators of crime and hold them accountable. For a criminal, accountability is terrible, and as a result, anyone they perceive as an authority figure, whether that be a teacher or a parent, will always have a negative perception. Unless they confess, one offender is held accountable for explanations for why they behaved as they did. Their after-the-fact statements are usually intended to gain sympathy and minimize responsibility. They focus on people and circumstances outside themselves. Unfortunately, may seasoned justice and mental health professionals do not analyze these statements further and take them at their face value.

Incredible Facts about the Criminal Brain

If a criminal does not have enough excuses for a crime that allow them to escape accountability, mental health providers today strive to provide more. When it comes to understanding the reasons behind a criminal's compulsion to commit a crime, there are lots of doubts and confusion. Perhaps some of this confusion could be eradicated if we adopt a more biological approach. The brain's normal operations are constituted by several parts working together in harmony. For the criminal, some of these parts are different in size when compared to the average person, causing them to act differently from the rest of us. Studies have found that two parts of the brain fought all the low are significantly smaller in people with antisocial personality disorder who act violently and become repeat offenders.

One of those parts was 18% smaller in antisocial people compared to ordinary people. The frontal lobe controls decision-making, emotions, and purposeful behaviors; criminals may have less authority over these functions. A study of psychopaths discovered that a component of that ammunition, the lot containing a brain region responsible for human emotion, had a volume almost 80% smaller than an average individual.

Consumers could be to blame, while most criminals do not have brain tumors. Some criminals have been found to have cancer which probably contributed to their undeniable actions. In 1966, Charles Whitman, who murdered 16 people at the University of Texas before being shot dead by police, was one of the most notorious of these individuals. Whitman had been suffering from excruciating migraines before the attack. With that, he had many rational thoughts and suicide notes.

Neurotransmitters are chemicals in our brains that deliver signals and cause reactions, such as arousal or trigger memory. Researchers found that some criminal brains have different levels of neurotransmitters than a normal brain. Serotonin at the proper levels keeps you from acting aggressively, and they are the first to fluctuate in levels when you are frustrated. So, when someone's brain contains more of the chemical, the person may respond impulsively. Dopamine levels influence whether a person feels rewarded for an action. Dopamine levels increase when someone acts aggressively, skillfully, and well and is likely to do so again.

The psychopath's brain does not respond to facial expressions; especially those who commit violent crimes may not have brains that register several expressions on others' faces. Moreover, in experiments, researchers have found that people with antisocial personality disorders have low recognition of faces, showing fear and sadness. Antisocial people who fall into the category of psychopaths find it more challenging to know when the expression is sad. Psychopaths also have almost no reaction or expression of fear. Ordinary people's brains will become very active when they see a scared expression. This difference may be what keeps a psychopath from feeling remorse as they do not register that others feel pain and sadness.

Furthermore, a psychopath is also fearless. A psychopath's brain does not react with fear as frequently as ours do in a test of criminal psychopathy. Researchers have found that they lack the fear conditioning that causes the rest of us to be afraid. We know something terrible is coming. The average person can be conditioned, much like Pavlov's Dog to their back when they hear a particular sound in the case of fear conditioning. Many researchers play a particular tune before administering an electric shock to the brain and associating the tune with the shot. The typical response to the two is anxiety. The psychopath's brain, however, does not change when the song plays; this lack of anxiety, teaching, and the consequences of their actions can make psychopaths perilous criminals.

The rational side of the irrational side communicates too much. The corpus Coliseum is the bridge in the brain that connects the rational left side with the rational right side in the criminal psychopath. This bundle of fibers is longer and thinner than the average person. It also seems to have more activity, meaning more communication between than the standard facility could be a good thing. The increased vacation causes psychopaths to be divided between the rational and the irrational. This division often leads to more impulsive behavior, and as such, psychopaths have more difficulty thinking through the consequences of their actions in a wholly rational way.

With that said, nature vs. mature nurture has always been a massive debate among criminologists. Still, research supports the idea that many criminal brains are genetically prone to aggressive or illegal behavior. Some criminals are a product of their environments and come from the use of homes or bad neighborhoods, but a large sum of murderers was raised in relatively conflict-free households. Criminals were not forced to commit these crimes, but their brains were more inclined to criminal acts than the brain of an average human. It also explains a criminal from a loving, wealthy upbringing can commit horrible violent crimes.

Teen brains are not fully formed yet. However, many teenagers can be tried as adults in most US states. Their brains are fully developed, yet reasoning and judgment are now known to mature throughout the teen years and into a person's winnings. When compared to adults, teenagers are more impulsive, more susceptible to peer pressure, less likely to look at the long-term consequences of their actions, and less able to think of ways out of bad situations. Aggression also peaked in the teenage years, which means that a violent teen may not be a violent adult. Most teenagers grow out of their violent phases. Many critics say that prisons should never be used for teenagers since it is likely that their brains will never develop further in the strict environment of a jail.

Are jobs not enough? People would dispute that working in support was a license to live responsibly. For decades sociologists and criminologists appointed unemployment as the leading cause of crime. Because of criminality, architects and rehabilitation houses have long contended that equipping the offenders with job skills and helping them find jobs reduces recidivism, and lack of employment, whether because of a lack of job skills. The other reason explains little about crime causation throughout the United States. Thousand people lost jobs as employment opportunities in the towns were disseminated. These individuals struggle with numerous problems after joblessness, but there is no evidence that most turn to crime.

Many offenders have job skills and stable jobs. Nonetheless, some became financially distilled because they lacked self-discipline, and spent all their money. Many people earning years worth of money spend it freely on whatever they want for they see no need to manage their finances. They are as undisciplined as financially as they are in other areas of life.

Throughout the United States, thousands of excellent job training and job placement programs are designed to help offenders live responsibly. In an article on November 8, 2016, Delaware Way, a community newspaper, described a correction program as a second chance for offenders while they worked on Howard when the restaurant was founded in 2000, and the scolding program was described as the first of its kind to offer these services.

All too often, with vocational training and job placement, criminals who are employed continue to commit crimes they steal from the jobs they hold for the user. Newly acquired skills to enter new arenas to commit crimes, becoming a proficient carpenter is of little value if the person steals from the job site, fails to show up for work, overcharges for quality materials, and fails to stand behind his work when problems arise.

Scientific studies show that a large majority of convicted criminals have some sort of psychological issue or problem in their brains, which has been shown to affect their behavior. To figure out who would be the most likely to do criminal acts in the first place, their brain must be analyzed to see if there are some early warning signs. As I have attempted to illustrate in this section of my research, many of these issues are biological and psychological in nature.

Alternatively, one may rely on the insights of neuroscience to understand criminals and criminality. Neuroscience is the study of the nervous system. Criminals have a very unorderly and stressful nervous system which shows in brain scans. This helps investigators catch and track down criminals.

A criminal mind contains gaps because of stress and certain spots of the brain which shows investigators if the suspect is guilty or not. Investigators can see certain specifications in each according to stress amounts and physiological reasons plus actions. Today, we're being presented with evidence that the brains of certain kinds of criminals are different from the rest of the population. While this can improve our understanding of criminal behavior, this also creates moral challenges about whether and how society should use this knowledge to use against crime. Neuroscience is still in its beginning, but the study of the brain's effect on human behavior may have a huge impact on the judicial system in the future.

Chapter 2

Nature v/s Nurture: Are Criminals Born or Made?

What makes a criminal? This is the question that I seek a plausible answer for. Criminality refers to the act of carrying out a crime, and the therapist has come up with speculations and reasons regarding why individuals perpetrate criminal acts.

The two primary illustrations lie in hereditary and natural components, which identify with the nature vs. nurture debate. Criminality has existed for as long as civilization, has exemplified in the story of Cain killing his sibling. The inquiry then becomes, -- are criminals born? Certainly not. Committing a crime is most likely not something one is born with; nevertheless, it occurs over time because of certain situations or circumstances that life tosses at an individual, such as family-related problems, the environment that one grows up in, and social causes.

Being locked up inside one's self can be a very lonely place. We look at men and women in prison and focus on their crimes. Criminals are depicted as being confined to their minds and how society views and treats them as a result of the heinous acts they have committed throughout their lives. People don't understand the difficulty that convicts face trying to change their lives to become productive in society and the daily struggle they have inside of themselves. Why do we make certain assumptions, and why are we biased? For example, why is that when we look at a man with a tattoo, and automatically assume he is from prison? Why do we assume that they are dangerous if someone commits a crime?

Crime and biological explanations focus more on the connection between genetics and crime. Relying on actual genetics, seen daily, is not enough to know if that person will become or is a criminal. Having bad genes does not necessarily make you violent or ferocious. It is more than just genes that define who is a criminal and who is not. It may be based on the situation they might be in. Everyone is unique in their way and has their own way of dealing with different problems.

Situations and circumstances in families can result in an individual's criminal choices. Children growing up in abuse are more likely to be criminals because they grow up with a lot of hate that they do not know how to deal with. One way they learn how to cope with their feelings is to be violent. Kids who have been exploited and misused are more likely to be criminals because they grow up with a significant amount of detest, which they do not know how to deal with. Therefore, one approach for adapting to the way they feel is to be vicious towards other people. Another related issue is lacking financial means that can cause innocent, law-abiding people to become a criminal.

When someone is committing a crime, what is going through their minds? What triggers them to commit a murder or violent crime? There are many theories on why criminals commit these heinous crimes. As far as most judicial systems are concerned, we recognize that those facts are not enough. Personality is the relatively persisting, distinctive, unified, and usable set of psychological characteristics that result from people's temperaments interacting with their ethnic and developmental experiences. Crime is the symbolic manifestation of tensions and conflicts within an individual's mind. Each individual holds a different personality, which in turn, causes them to respond to identical situations in different ways.

Our personality consists of three interacting components: the id, ego, and superego, with each having a different and specified purpose. The id is the natural crude material of our demeanor and nature; it speaks to our drives and senses for gaining life-supporting necessities and life's delights. Whereas the superego is the component of the personality that is responsible for a person's moral and ethical compass. According to Freud, an overdeveloped superego is thought to be the cause of much deviance. This indicates that persons with overdeveloped superegos feel guilty for no cause and want to be punished for it. So, committing crimes is a method of obtaining such desired punishment and relieves the guilt. A person commits a crime so that they can get punished.

The fact is that people who are not born criminals, environment, and genes, can cause misbehavior. Genes aren't the only factor that impacts who we are and who we become; we should pay attention to the prison environment and its mindset in a person.

What makes people want to commit crimes? Are criminals any different from us? Does committing a crime to mean something is wrong with you and that you suffer from a psychological problem? Do all criminals have the same kind of personality? Is a criminal born or made? Questions like this and many more will be elaborated on throughout this paper.

The first question I want to focus on is, "Are criminals any different than us?" The criminals tended to be more careless, under the average intelligence level, and less emotionally stable than non-criminal citizens. Using Sinha's data from the case study shows that criminals are different from us.

The second question I want to focus on is, "how do criminals become criminals?" Learned behaviors of aggression and violence can lead to crime. If someone plays violent video games so much to the point where it becomes a part of their life, it may become hard to separate what is acceptable and what is not. As a result, their worldview begins to differ greatly from that of the average man or woman.

Furthermore, another example can be a child coming from an abusive family where they were used to being beaten around. Because the child is beaten regularly, they may believe that it is normal and acceptable in life. Dr. Boyd's findings in her work prove that the reasoning for criminals to commit a crime is not only learned but also biological. People with biological disorders, such as mental disorders, tend to be a large portion of criminals.

Additionally, those individuals may believe that their lives are unfair and may be struggling to get back on track. Also, there's always the possibility that their mental disorder causes them not to think clearly. Nevertheless, according to

The third question I want to elaborate on is, "Are criminals born or made?" Criminals are not born; they are made because they develop their mannerisms no matter what genes they have.

In conclusion, there is indeed evidence that criminals are different from us. Sudhinta Sinha's work proves that criminals tend to be more careless, under the average intelligence level, and less emotionally stable than non-criminal citizens. Furthermore, criminals become criminals because they typically have mental disorders. Dr. Natalie Boyd's studies have shown that most criminals have mental disorders that cause them to commit criminal acts. Moreover, criminals are made, not born. Research by Professor Jim Fallon proved that specific genes are commonly found in criminals, but some people exist who have them but are not criminals. This shows that criminals are developed, not born to be criminals. Criminal psychology has led us to understand why people turn to be criminals to understand better how to prevent more crimes from being committed. We come up with the fact that people aren't born criminals, and it is the environment and their genes that make them misbehave and get awry.

Nevertheless, our genes aren't the only factor that impacts who we are or even how we might behave in a state of affairs that has happened to us. It is also the environment we exist in and the people with whom we have connections, which implies who we are as a person or even if we might commit a criminal act.

A highly debated topic concerns whether criminals commit crimes because of social pressure or an individual urge. The strain theory supports crime as a social pressure because, as Frank Schmalleger suggests in Criminology.

Today, crime is an adaptive behavior that coincides with problems caused by frustration or unpleasant social surroundings. Also, culture conflict theory states the cause of delinquent behavior is because different social classes have conflicting morals of what is appropriate or proper behavior (Schmalleger 228). Other people believe blaming crime on the economy or where they grew up is an excuse for criminals instead of making them take responsibility for their actions, as stated by CQ writer Peter Katel. These different views started with statistics taken on crime in the early 1800s. Andre Michel Guerry of France was one of the first examiners of "the moral health of nations" in the early It is doubtful this issue will ever be settled since there are too many pros and cons to each side.

However, while specialists dispute this, crime is not stopping. There needs to be a way, or possibly several ways, to reduce criminal activity. It is doubtful that criminal activity will ever be put to an end. The same is to be said about why people commit a crime but knowing if it is done socially or individually can help with the fight against it. In the end, individuals should take responsibility for their actions, but in today's world, most people are not taught this; thus, crime is regarded as a social activity by countless experts.

Instead of proposing that criminals commit crimes due to social behavior, another view on the subject is they do it out of their own will. Stanton E. Samenow states in "Inside the Criminal Mind 16" that social sciences circulate the outlook that humans come into the world "like a lump of clay to be shaped by external forces."

This does nothing except give criminals an excuse for committing crimes. It is better said by Samenow when he says, "This view renders us all victims!" Something that happened in the past would be found to be a "reason" for the behavior. For example, if the parents of a criminal were strict, it would be the parents' fault because they were too harsh on the child. This gives the parents minimal ways of raising their children since if they are strict, they are at fault, but if they allow their kids to do as they please, they will experiment with drugs and other forbidden activities, which could lead to worse crimes.

Crime can be looked at as a social act in numerous ways. The most obvious one in the world today is gangs. A couple of reasons a person joins a gang is for "respect" or to have a "family" they never had. Also, if a youngster has parents or older siblings involved with crime and/or gangs, the young person is more inclined to follow in their footsteps.

Furthermore, some people who grow up in crime-filled neighborhoods believe the only way to make a living is by selling drugs or stealing. This goes along well with Cozic's statement in Gangs, Opposing Viewpoints 42,

"Under capitalism, people are taught that competition is a good thing, that there are two types of people in the world, winners and losers. To be a winner, you have to do whatever it takes to get what you want. If you don't, you're a loser."

Many of today's criminals are hard-headed people who do not have failed as an option; thus, gangs and organized crime are created to ensure they are "winners," at least in their book. Moreover, crime can be blamed on any social establishment (Saenow 12). "Schools have been singled out as forcing into crime youngsters who don't fit the academic mold...Newspapers, television, and the movies have been charged with glamorizing crime" (Samenow 12).

This is a powerful statement because nowadays, media significantly influences the younger society. Young people today believe breaking the law is "cool" because that is what all the "cool" people do. They are also taught at a young age through school and the media that listening to parents is "lame," causing sons and daughters to disobey their parent's rules and grow up without any humility because they are taught to be above everybody, including the law. Finally, there are many social factors in the world right now that contribute to criminal behavior.

An occurrence is going on today that causes debate is the economy. Do people commit crimes because they have fallen upon rough times, or do they decide that they feel it is a better way of supporting themselves? The social crimes supporters may say because of the limited number of jobs and vast unemployment rate, many people have no choice but to commit crimes. As said by Samenow 13, "Financial pressures are said to push despondent people over the edge." He also says economic problems force mothers to return to work, causing the children to have less supervision and making them more vulnerable to peer pressure.

On the other hand, crime rates also increase during good times, and most of the lower class and broken homes people are law-abiding citizens (Samenow 13). A good or bad economy is no excuse for committing a crime. It is challenging to withstand the temptation of stealing or other crimes, especially when everyone around is doing it successfully.

Lastly, in today's day and age, crime is more of social activity since what people see around them tends to influence their actions in the future. A fix to this problem would have to start when people are young because it is easier to mold them into learning to avoid crime and be an individual or a leader, not a follower. Crime is a social affair now, but with hard work and dedication, youngsters can be kept off the path of crime and become morally sound, responsible adults.

Chapter 3

What Makes a Criminal a Criminal?

Can anyone become a criminal? As stated earlier, the core work of criminologists is answering and understanding these questions, consider the notion that any person could become a criminal and, in so doing, consider the initial question. In formulating a response to the aforementioned question, this chapter will outline a range of theories that attempt to describe human behavior concerning criminal behavior, given the complexities of behavior. Several theories will be considered as no single theory of behavior can account for all the complexities and range of criminal behavior. The theories range from social-control to classical, biological, personality, impulse, and cognitive theories. The multiple factors influencing people's behavior, including criminal behavior, are also considered. These factors include family circumstances, personality, and mental health issues. Lastly, we will take into consideration the roles that society plays in defining and contributing to people engaging in criminal behaviors.

Before considering the overall question, it is crucial to define criminal behavior. Defining criminal behavior is complex. The definition of criminal behavior is any person 'guilty of crime' (Webster's universal dictionary & thesaurus, 2007). This definition demonstrates the wide-ranging behaviors considered criminal.

Having defined criminal behavior and its broad terms, the explanation of that behavior needs to be equally comprehensive.

***

There may be many reasons influencing this phenomenon, including socioeconomic and the limited resources associated with this (including less money and fewer services).

However, the view that crime pays well and many commit crime for a lucrative lifestyle is simplistic and unlikely to explain the range in criminal behavior and circumstances surrounding that behavior. It has been noted that while some may view crime as an avenue to gaining a lifestyle, crime could also cause significantly impaired lifestyles. These are consistent with the classical theory.

Self-control is believed to be learned in childhood. These studies have demonstrated that different parenting techniques can contribute to individuals' ability to manage their self-control. One or both parents can reduce delinquency if they provide the child with relevant structure. If there is no structure or inconsistencies, this can lead to antisocial behavior, increasing the chances of someone committing a crime.

***

Research has noted that some people who have committed crimes appear not to have a conscience. This is associated with the value system or the individuals' beliefs relating to what they perceive as good and bad behavior. The personality of these criminals significantly influences this notion, particularly personality types demonstrating borderline personality disorders and sociopathic or psychopathic tendencies.

Personality theory considers antisocial behavior in terms of the individual's composition of personality traits. In these people, crime-related behavior may have become a long-established pattern, and the person believes that this is the way to behave, possibly due to what they want or need.

***

Taking into consideration the insights that all these theories have to offer, various theories can be utilized to consider criminal behavior. These include explanations of the social milieu and individual characteristics which may lead a person to commit a crime and thus become a criminal. This chapter has considered social theory, classical theory, biological theory, personality theory, impulse theory, and cognitive theory in the context of people's criminal behavior.

Considering these theories, it becomes evident that any person may commit a crime and that no theory adequately accounts for all criminal behavior or who may become a criminal. Given that not all crimes committed result in imprisonment, reflecting the wide range of criminal behaviors, it is unlikely that any theory can address all aspects. It is also essential to consider the factors leading people who do not commit a crime. This assists in identifying the protective factors or factors that prevent people from committing a crime.

Criminologists agree that the gender gap in crime, which refers to the low level of female offending in relation to males, is a universal fact, but this avenue of research opens up the question as to why this gap exists in the first place. The answer to such a question would be complex and would have to investigate several factors, including the causes of female crime versus causal factors for men. Are they the same or distinct, and can traditional social theories explain female crime and the gender gap? Steffensmeier and Allen (1996) discuss the long-standing matter concerning whether theories of crime developed by male criminologists looking at a male crime can explain female crime.

It has been argued that traditional theories are male-specific and not applicable to female crime. Schwartz and Steffensmeier (2008) propose that the traditional theories are essentially gender-neutral and can be used to explain female and male crime at a general level. However, they do concede that better understanding could be achieved by a gendered approach accounting for the difference between the lives of men and women that shape offending patterns.

Chapter 4

What Causes Criminal Behavior

Criminologists have come up with many different answers and theories about why individuals commit crimes and the factors that pertain to criminal behaviors. Even though there are several answers, each answer and theory help the legal system deter such criminal activity. One of the most costly forms of crime—the white – collar— shows many distinct characteristics that can be placed in a criminal profile. Based on the existing theories and profiles that criminology offers us, a determination can be made as to why individuals commit white-collar crimes.

Individual Engagement in Criminal Activity

Crime takes place daily, and for criminologists, the question is why people engage in criminal behavior. Most crimes take lots of planning, while others only happen with no thought process. As varied as crimes may be, the factors that may cause crime to occur are just as diverse. Some may think that poverty is the main root of criminal behavior. However, this explanation falls short when we take into account the many wealthy individuals involved in criminal activity and white-collar crimes. Some may still believe that poverty plays a huge role since many individuals look for a better life and try to take the easy way out.

While poverty does seem to be a significant factor as to why individuals commit crimes, crimes are committed for other reasons, too. These can range from social, cultural, and economic reasons. Socially, individuals commit crimes due to influences from peers, while cultural reasons include hatred towards another group. For some individuals, the factors inciting their criminal behavior may be psychological problems. As such, several different factors can contribute to what causes individuals to commit crimes, and such nuance must be taken into account when investigating a particular criminal act.

Theoretical Explanations

Further into history, criminologists have examined even more reasoning behind individuals committing crimes. Studies have shown that other factors have contributed to an individual committing a crime. With more and more studies conducted, theories have been discovered as to why crime exists. These are known as General Strain, Self-control, and Life Course.

Robert Agnew developed General Strain Theory. He explains that crime is caused by the "strain" that each individual faces throughout their lives (Agnew, 1992, pp. 47-87).

Chesney-Lind and Sheldon elucidate further,

"Strain or pressure is placed upon certain persons in the society to engage in nonconformist rather than conformist conduct." (1998, p.83)

There are many instances where individuals do not use legitimate methods to reach their goals. Not using legitimate methods, especially when money is a concern, can trigger criminal behavior to cope with the strain. A person's personality and emotions can also lead to criminal behaviors. Agnew showed how the more an individual is strained, the better chance the individual will resort to criminal behavior in order to cope.

The Self Control Theory was created by Gottfredson and Hirschi, and in contrast to the Strain theory, it describes how one's lack of self-control can cause one to commit crimes because one does not create a healthy coping skill. Typically, individuals that have no self-control seek out other avenues to find gratification. This type of behavior over time leads to illegal decisions such as drug use, prostitution, or even gambling.

The Life Course Theory was developed by Sampson and Laub and was designed to understand an individual's behavior throughout their life.

The theory also shows the different risk factors throughout an individual's life and how the course of a person's life effects their criminal behaviors.

All three of the theories discussed present different thoughts on why someone would engage in criminal activity. However, all three theories have a similar conclusion; criminal activity can occur if something changes in an individual over time.

Prevent and Discourage Criminal Behavior

Preventing or discouraging criminal behavior is difficult no matter how anyone in society looks at it. No one is perfect, and everything does not always stay the same. Many individuals can handle the changes of life and the challenges that it presents, while others seek new avenues, including criminal activity.

In my opinion, perhaps the most optimal way to prevent and discourage criminal behavior is for society to instill the proper morals in people when they are still small children. Stricter laws ought to be passed, and penalties need to be more challenging. If individuals feel that they will either not get caught or only receive something like probation or community service, criminal activity will continue to thrive.

Another important way to control criminal activity is to educate society and teach them the laws and what to look for. Still, one must be realistic and realize that criminal activity will probably never be eliminated. Still, with the knowledge of harsher penalties, people might think twice about reverting themselves to a life of crime to achieve wealth or just gratification.

Individuals ought to realize, also, the challenges that criminals face once they get caught. One of the most difficult aspects of the prison system is the stigmatization that comes after release. This stigmatization against minorities makes re-integration back into society extremely difficult, especially in the labor market. Large populations of convicts are men, and this has a negative effect on the stability of families.

Social stigma is one of the common problems which ex-convicts are facing today. This is one of the reasons why they cannot change themselves for the better because of the labels being imposed on them. In other words, social stigma imposed on the ex-convicts hinders their willingness to change for the better because of the bad impression on them and other people thinks...show more content...

Therefore, social acceptance is appreciated when one is welcomed by one's fellow for what he in or what he believes in. However, Baumester and Bushman (2008) suggested that social exclusion is considered to be the opposite of acceptance. It is a concept that refers to the process in which individuals are being prevented by others from forming or keeping a social bond with them. If an individual experiences such a dilemma, then he is socially excluded.

"This year, over 600,000 people will be released from prison, and many millions will be returning to their communities from shorter stints in jails" (2).

With this statement, would you feel comfortable continuing to live in your neighborhood? Or immediately pack up your family and move elsewhere. Ex-convicts have many challenges when released from prison, which include finding employment, overcoming their troubled past, and facing the stigma of how society views them.

Do you know if any of your family members have been convicted? You ever wonder how hard it was for an ex-convict to find a job without being turned down because of their past.

In the past ten years, ex-convicts all have been experiencing this problem, impacting hundreds of ex-convicts.

Another problem facing ex-convicts is finding a job. Not many business owners want to hire an ex-convict. Many business owners try to avoid this as much as possible because they want to avoid the problems that could come along with the ex-convicts. But what they do not understand is that they could be passing up potential good committed workers. Many times, to stop the problem is to simply avoid it over all to prevent it. Many business owners aren't willing to take the risk due to the thought of being robbed under their noses.

Furthermore, many ex-convicts have problems fitting into the world, yet alone being rejected for their past decisions. In order to solve the problem of ex-cons, business owners need to be informed about ex-convicts, understand what the ex-convicts, and have business owners talk to other business owner about their experience.

First, to solve the problem of the ex-cons not being able to find a job, business owners need to be informed about the situation of the ex-convicts. Business owners need to see this as a problem to solve rather than to ignore.

Overall, addressing the problem of prisoner reintegration is vital for the future of our country. The inherent duty of our justice system is to rehabilitate and then reintegrate criminal offenders, yet today we still have high rates of recidivism in the United States. Overall, we as a nation have imprisoned far too many citizens, and our prisons are being filled to the brim. Because of the high rates of imprisonment and failures in our prison system, many Americans are not properly equipped to be reintegrated back into society and are likely to contribute to the high recidivism rates. Overall, the formation of a national reintegration program would be beneficial in that it can lower the rates...show more content...

This would essentially include family assistance/ counseling, addiction counseling, and welfare assistance. According to Wiemer, "[Ex-convicts] determined to change their lives, consequently, relied more heavily on familial ties."

The families of criminal offenders play a huge role in reintegration and are a prime source of both emotional and physical support for the men and women who decide to turn their lives around. The program would work to ensure that these familial bonds are strengthened or repaired by offering family counseling. By doing such, much of the burden of reintegration of a prisoner can be shifted off the public and onto the immediate family. Accounts of recidivism are prominent among substance abusers. Often times this is what bars prisoners from repairing their lives through true rehabilitation.

Lastly, the program would also work to assist prisoners with obtaining some form of welfare. While providing "cash assistance" has been argued to be counterproductive, it has far more potential for good when utilized correctly. Poverty is one of the greatest factors contributing to recidivism. If we equip impoverished prisoners with some form of conditional welfare, we can ease the transitional period of him/her while reducing their risk of reoffending.

This is feasible in the sense that the program would not actually deal with any monetary assistance on its own. Instead, it would work to ensure that convicts become eligible for the many programs already in place. In this way, the program would be effective in reducing recidivism due to poverty. Adjusting to life after incarceration can be a very long and difficult process to overcome. There are several obstacles people face when returning home for the first time in years. Most people generally come home to nothing and have to try to make a life out of it.

An ex-con may face stigma, a lack of opportunities, and the constant risk of recidivism. Recidivism is the ongoing cycle of incarceration. The ex-con continues to be in and out of prison because they cannot successfully re-transition into society. This topic is worth investigating because recidivism is a current problem in the United States, and it usually takes place because the justice system fails to prepare their inmates for what life will be like. Rehabilitation is key because there is a lack of success in offenders returning home.

Young adults should be aware of recidivism because they can easily be sucked into the system, and this can happen to them. They can find themselves in a position where they end up in prison and fall victim to recidivism. Questions that will guide this research include:

1. What resources are available for those who are trying to re-enter society after prison?

2. How does stereotypes and stigma affect how they adapt and thrive in society?

3. What is the correlation between lack of opportunities and recidivism?

4. How does rehabilitation contribute to lower recidivism rates vs. prison?

Chapter 5

Insight into Criminal Behavior

Juvenile exposure to criminal behavior increases the chances that those individuals will also engage in criminal behavior. Research gives us insight into preventing or reducing criminality and rehabilitating law violators who engage in criminal behavior.

What causes people to commit crimes? Interdisciplinary criminology gives us a better understanding of several fields of study to better understand crime. Influential factors that influence criminal behaviors are psychological, sociological, and biological. How do we help rehabilitate criminals? Each approach agrees on a criminal's devotion to aggressive behavior, but they differ in their conclusions.

Psychological involves personality, addressing specific felt needs, and defective mental processes. Sociology deals with the cause and control of criminality. The social structures, cultural values, peer groups, and family all make up this approach. The biological approach deals with a person's biological makeup, such as heredity, neurotransmitter dysfunction, and brain abnormalities, as significant components in criminal behavior.

Each approach consists of different methods of control, expression of behavior, and influences on criminal behavior. Situational and environmental factors provide a setting and opportunity for crime to occur. Cultural forces help us analyze the context for occurring crimes. Phenomenology determines the personal meaning that a crime holds for the offender.

Researchers use different approaches to their theories, but each contributes something to our understanding of the critical components of development. A contribution to an individual's development begins in the womb and continues to develop well into adulthood. Many considerations should be factored into determining the causation of crime and delinquency.

Early psychodynamic development, processing, and cognition fall under the psychological theories concerning crime. Sociological theories locate the source of criminality outside of a person. Forensic psychology is where the justice system and psychology intertwine. Understanding these legal principles determines the competence of stand trial, custody, and visitation and how to interact with individuals that have committed crimes.

Environmental psychology focuses on the interplay between humans and their surroundings. Natural, social, built, learning, and informational environments play a part in this interdisciplinary field. Human performance is affected by envy because children don't get to choose their environment. Child development theories have emerged throughout the 20th Century regarding Influronmental stress. The family environment determines a child's well-being. Families that exhibit a stimulating home environment, a caring and nurturing environment, and consistent discipline are more likely to produce a child with these characteristics. A family that does not offer that environment to their child is more likely to produce a child with aggressive and criminal behavior. One statistic proves that children who have been abused or neglected are at a 50 % greater risk of engaging in criminal activity.

In children and adolescents, the environment plays a vital role in influencing their behavior Influences on child development are complex. Interactions among family members are influential in behavior. Understanding the cognitive, emotional, social, and educational growth that children experience is crucial for society.

Psychoanalytic theories deal with conflicts inside the person that produces criminal behavior. This orientation addresses the moral sense that leads to an individual's choices. Another primary psychoanalytical theory of criminal behavior attributes criminal and asocial tendencies to failure to develop psychologically in early childhood. The causes of crime and delinquency can be understood through two significant schools of criminological Theory; classical and vivacious. People who choose to commit a crime fall under the classical Theory. The environmental influences on a behavior fall under the positive Theory. Biological and environmental factors play an integral role in juvenile crime.

The classical theory of crime involves the rationality of human nature and free will. The potential pleasure or reward from illegal acts outweighs the punishment for a criminal. Ivan Pavlov discovered this learning process, significantly influencing psychologists' schools of thought regarding behaviors. Classical conditioning does not consider thoughts, feelings, or emotions when determining behavior. The process in classical conditioning begins with an unconditional stimulus automatically triggering a response. A response occurs naturally, which is called an unconditioned response. A conditioned stimulus is neutral until it is associated with the unconditional stimulus. The trigger is a conditioned response, a learned response to a neutral stimulus.

Several theorists have focused on how environmental interaction influences behavior throughout a child's development. Some theories do not consider one's thoughts or feelings. Experiences in childhood do tend to shape individuals. Crime can be attractive when it promises big rewards, and little effort is needed in the classical approach. Our constitution is based on classical Theory.

Phobias are sometimes formed through classical conditioning. An example of classical conditioning would be trainers teaching their pets. This conditioning is used in training K-9 dogs to search for specific substances. This technique can also be helpful in the treatment of phobias or anxiety. A positive environment can help individuals overcome fears and anxieties to be rehabilitated. The application of operant and classical conditioning is applied behavioral analysis (ABA). This method can help change behaviors by assessing behavior and environment and help implement intensive behavioral interventions.

Operant conditioning occurs through a reward system for good behavior and punishment for bad behavior. This gives an individual the association between their behavior and consequences for their behavior by B. F. Skinner's Theory. This conditioning is around us in our day-to-day world. As children and adults, operant conditioning is around us at school, home, and work. The possibility of praise can increase behavior or decrease behavior depending on the situation. If there are some undesirable behaviors, the thought of punishment may reduce the disruptive behavior.

However, some theories look at genetic and environmental influences that affect criminal behavior. With this Theory, individuals learn criminal behavior from family, culture, and environment. The surroundings of an individual can reinforce criminal tendencies. The first core concept within this Theory is people learn by observing others. The second is internal mental states which are an essential part of this process. And third, this Theory acknowledges that just because something has been learned doesn't mean a behavior change will occur. Attention, retention, reproduction, and motivation encourage appropriate behaviors in the observational and modeling process.

The General Strain Theory deals with circumstances in which stress leads to anger and crime. Anger results from blaming adversity on others. This implies that when an adolescent blames some stress on another person, they might get angry and commit delinquent acts. Negative social experiences contribute mainly to criminal behavior about crime and opportunity. This strain has a severe impact on crime. Strain is influential when determining the outcome of an individual's life, goals, success, achieving "status," or money.

Controlled Theory is the opposite of the "why" theories and focuses on why people don't get into criminal behavior. This Theory of moral development involves socialization, character, and the development of conscience, and each of these controls antisocial behaviors. Tendencies toward anger, anxiety, and guilt can push individuals toward criminal behavior.

Sigmund Freud focused primarily on mental disorders and stressed the importance of childhood events and experiences. His Theory outlined development steps that play a role in an adult's personality and behavior. If one of these stages is not developed successfully, the effects will surface later in life. Erik Erikson's Theory was focused on human growth throughout one's lifespan.

Freud believed that the psyche included three components. First is the instinctual drive, a person's unconscious. The second component is the super-ego, representing a person's consciousness and how they internalize societal norms and morality. The third would be the ego, the conscious, which integrates the instinctual drives and the super-ego's prohibitions. Freud strongly believed this conflict to be at the heart of neurosis.

Much evidence proves that our criminal justice system includes many individuals with psychological problems. These individuals don't want help until they get into trouble or commit a crime. Genetics is not the sole reason behind criminal behavior but is a critical factor in these determinations. As we begin to have more research and data, we become more knowledgeable about how genetics and environmental factors affect criminal behavior.

The theories, studies, and approaches to understanding how these develop into criminal behavior give us insight into how to improve the systems in place to better serve the needs of society in regard to reducing crime and getting to the root of the problems. Behavioral patterns and tendencies are activated by neurochemicals in certain parts of the brain. Neurotransmitters directly influence neurons that affect behavior. These are chemicals that transmit messages from one nerve cell to another.

Serotonin is a neurochemical that plays a vital role in the personality traits of anxiety, depression, and bipolar disorder). Studies prove that serotonin is one of the most critical central neurotransmitters involved in impulsive aggression. Low serotonin levels have been linked to impulsive behavior or emotional aggression. Serotonin is directly related to aggression and can also lead to antisocial or criminal behavior. Another neurotransmitter associated with aggression is dopamine. Neurotransmitters directly influence neurons that affect behavior. When dopamine is lacking in the brain, it affects thinking and emotional reactions. Suppose abnormal neurotransmitter activity, mood, thoughts, and pain are affected. Neurotransmitters not being balanced can also cause problems at work and in daily responsibilities. Having imbalances in these chemicals have lasting effects on areas of attention, impulse control, and overactivity. Addictions can be linked to these imbalances and lead to criminal activity. Alcoholism initially helps control stress but later reduces muscle control and reaction time.

Mental conditions crop up through various behaviors and interfere with an individual's coping ability. Criminals with mental disorders are affected by their perceptions, decision-making abilities, reasoning, and beliefs. The natural part of criminal behavior is in conjunction with disease or disorder of the nervous system and can explain some uncontrollable behaviors they exhibit. The majority of the psychiatric syndromes include abnormal levels of neurotransmitters. Genetics and brain chemistry give us insight into biological predisposition and environmental conditions and how each of these plays off of each other. There are genetic and physical factors that lead a person to criminal behavior.

Chapter 6

Rehabilitating Our Criminals

America releases 600,000 prisoners each year but does little to prepare them for work or improve their unlawful habits. However, not surprisingly, within three years, many ex-convicts are re-arrested (Solomon et al. 38). People who have already spent time in prison or jail move back to some of America's poorest neighborhoods to terrorize neighbors who can ill afford the costs of crime. United States prisons are ineffective in protecting society and rehabilitating criminals to return to society.

A new Urban Institute study, "From Prison to Home: The Dimensions and Consequences of Prisoner Reentry," provides frightening documentation of America's failure to improve the prospects for released prisoners. According to the Urban Institute study, fewer prisoners have gotten an education and drug treatment behind bars within the past decade, while more have violated parole terms. Many ex-convicts are released with no money and a lousy record, making it difficult for ex-convicts to succeed. The Urban Institute study states, "Despite tough-on-crime rhetoric, over

100,000 people a year get released without any supervision, and per-convict spending has fallen for those who remain monitored." Many ex-convicts are forced to live in poverty and continue to live a "dark life," which often makes it difficult to find a full-time job and return to their families with adequate care and mentality to support them.

However, prisons protect society from harsh criminals who commit violent felonies against society. U.S. government official Donald Taylor states, "Over the past ten years, prisons have maintained their essential task: keeping United States citizens safe from convicted felons." The overall purpose of a prison is to keep "bad" people away from society where they cannot commit violent acts against innocent people. Prisons are effective because they lock up the people who threaten society. According to the book Evaluation of Penal Measures, "The range for success in rehabilitation cases ranges from 30 percent success to 60 percent success". This study was taken over five years and shows rehabilitation positively impacted many prisoners once released into society.

Although the overall purpose of rehabilitation in prison has its positive aspects, the weaknesses of rehabilitation make prison time ineffective in protecting society. Rehabilitation may provide aid to some prisoners; however, many prisoners are still unaffected by the rehabilitation and leave prison in the same state of mind as the day they were sentenced. "Twenty-five percent of all prisoners released commit an additional crime within five years."

Prisons dramatically change the values and morals of a person; according to a book entitled, The Felon, "Persons who are sentenced to prison experience a sudden blow that hurls them outside society. It not only unravels their social ties; it stuns them and reduces their capacity and resolves to make the journey back into society". Prisons change people, and regardless of the rehabilitation offered to the convicts, many prisoners are impacted by their time in prison, which becomes apparent when released.

Fifty-five years ago, nineteen-year-old Rueben Fischer finished his job at Louie's Garage at nine o'clock pm. He began his four-block walk to his apartment as the sun was beginning to set on a beautiful day in June. Two blocks from his apartment, a man in his forties approached him and asked him for spare change. Rueben told the man he had no money and walked away. Reuben walked five more steps before being shot through his back and killed. The man took Reuben's life for a wallet with no money.

An older woman witnessed Reuben's death through her small shop window and was able to describe the felon to the police. The offender was a forty-five-year-old man who had just been released from prison for a previous murder. Prison did not rehabilitate or institute the proper time or punishment to keep this man from taking another innocent life. Reuben would possibly still be alive today if an ex-convict had not cruelly taken his life. Unfortunately, similar instances occur in our society constantly because prisons are not serving to keep society safe.

U.S. prisons are ineffective in protecting society and rehabilitating criminals to return to society. Statistics show that prison rehabilitation does impact the reduction of prisoners' reentry; however, many ex-convicts still continue to disobey society's norms and go against the nation's laws. Rehabilitation may protect society on a small scale; however, it will not successfully reintegrate all 600,000 men and women who leave correctional facilities each year.

In addition, convicts who have stolen, murdered, raped, or committed other wrongful acts against innocent people have affected many lives. Funding needs to be implemented to monitor prisoners individually to determine whether a convict is genuinely ready to be released into society.

What is the importance of having prisoner reentry programs for those released from prison? Two-thirds of released prisoners are re-arrested three years of release. One and a half million children have a Parent in Prison. Four million citizens have lost their right to vote. Men and women enter U.S. prisons with limited marketable work experience, low educational or vocational skills, and many health-related issues, ranging from mental health needs to substance abuse histories and high rates of infectious diseases.

When they leave prison, these challenges remain and affect neighborhoods, families, and society. Prisoner reentry is defined as "All activities and programming conducted to prepare ex-convicts to return safely to the community and live as law-abiding citizens." So what exactly do these programs consist of? In today's society, prisoners' rehabilitation before reentering society is mediocre at best. Most are just thrown back into the world with no warning or help other than being assigned to a probation officer. The question now is why and what can we do to change the way we treat released prisoners.

The prison system has been rapidly growing within the past decade, which means more people are being released from prison, aside from those on death row and serving life sentences. According to Jeremy Travis, "In 2002, more than 630,000 individuals left federal and state prison, compared with the 150,000 who made a similar journey 30 years ago". Mass Incarceration in America has brought about significant problems regarding prisoner reentry. So many people are going to jail at such an alarming rate which means that these people will also be released at an alarming rate. We then have to figure out how to integrate them back into society to lead daily, crime-free lives again. Travis asks how "to develop a jurisprudence of reintegration that can comfortably coexist with the disparate philosophies governing sentencing practices." Travis then argues that sentencing needs to be reformed, and a reintegration sentence system must be implemented.

This reintegration system must first include job security. Ex-cons must stop being discriminated against when it comes to obtaining a job. Upon release, each inmate must have a job set up and a safe and secure place to stay; these conditions must be met for release. Recent studies show that "between 75 and 80 percent of parolees remain jobless up to a year after being released from prison."

There are three main reasons why ex-convicts do not get hired: Selection, Transformation, or Credentials, all of which have to do with the idea that people who end up in prison do not want to work; or that prison changes inmates and makes them undesirable to the labor market; or that incarceration creates barriers that do not allow for employment. These factors will more than likely cause an ex-convict to become frustrated and return to a life of crime to make money.

To avoid this stigma, programs must be put in place that allows released prisoners to obtain employment easier. Even if that means they are required to go through a series of steps that will prove they are ready and able for employment, any motivated person will not mind going through these minor things. If anyone is unwilling, it shows that they aren't as motivated as they may have seemed before.

Jobs are not the only issue that prisoners face once released from jail; formerly incarcerated individuals also need extreme family support once released from prison. Those who do not have the support of their families are more likely to fall through the cracks and end up right back where they started. Families also face extreme stress when it comes to prisoner reentry.

The stress usually comes from some or all of these factors; housing, employment support, transportation, finances, or even childcare. "Given the stress suffered when assisting family members, both male and female participants expressed a desire for support programs that aid the family member in helping another individual in reentry;" a support group was formed.

Wives have also become widely affected by the mass incarceration of their husbands, resulting in them having to act as the head of the household. Prisoner wives often suffer from "loss of income, difficulty maintaining contact with the prisoner, deterioration in relationships, and social isolation." In 1965 Morris conducted a study the study included 469 wives of prisoners. The results were as follows: Slightly less than half of the prisoner wives experienced deterioration in their attitudes about marriage and plans for the future.

In addition, Morris asserted that wives perceived their husband's imprisonment as a crisis of family dismemberment more than a crisis of demoralization (shame and guilt). Loss of income was a major issue associated with the incarceration of a husband. To exacerbate these issues, prisoners' wives were expected to continue to support themselves, the prisoners, and their children, which was associated with tremendous strain and vulnerability.

Some may wonder what happens to those formerly incarcerated individuals who do not have wavering support from their families. Nine times out of ten, they become stuck with poverty, "poverty is the most prevalent in the lives of individuals who in communities most impacted by prisoner reentry." Mass reintegration of ex-prisoners takes an incredible toll on communities. In turn, they begin to disintegrate, "related to prisoner reentry, and mass incarceration leads us to conclude that as the return of ex-prisoners changes the other community structural factors, it culminates in the diminishing of the political, social, and economic ability of the community.

When the community is not given the tools and programs to help these people return safely to their neighborhoods and get back on track, it is more than likely that these individuals will return to crime, which is the last thing anyone wants. Support groups for families, mental health counseling sessions, educational courses, job-seeking skills workshops, and even programs to help incarcerated parents strengthen their relationships with their children are just some initiatives that must be introduced.

America has always had a problem with how it treats its prisoners and those being released from prison. Why are formerly incarcerated individuals still treated as incarcerated instead of ordinary everyday citizens? Two-thirds of released prisoners return to jail within a year to three years, mainly because they were not given the tools or programs to return to society when they were released.

They are constantly discriminated against when obtaining a job, whether it be because of selection, transformation, or credentials. This leads to them returning to a life of crime they were living before. Not only that, but families have a difficult time when it comes to coping with the stress of supporting these ex-convicts. There should be prisoner reentry programs not only for the former convicts but the families as well. They carry most of the burden of a loved one returning home from prison. Communities should also be allowed to put programs in place to help out these families and those returning, especially considering prisoners are being released just as often as they are being booked. If everyone works together and forms a solid plan and works to put these programs in place, there is no reason that we should have former prisoners falling through the cracks and returning to the system that failed them in the first place.

Rehabilitation in prison: Is it possible or a lost cause?

When people think about the men and women that occupy our prison system, It is for sure that one of the first things that come to their mind is not "rehabilitation" and the different programs that could be implemented in order to get these crooks mentally healthy and ready to be released back into society. More often than not, what does come to one's mind are the negative behaviors that got these men and women into the prison system in the first place. This punishment will be laid out for them, the long hours that are going to be spent thinking about what they have done to not only their lives but the lives of the individuals targeted and their families. It is easy to forget that these people are human and have the same character defects that most of us "normal" folk have, but we fail to realize that some people never really had a chance at a normal life from the very start.

In Rita Hayworth and the Shawshank Redemption, there was a lack of rehabilitation in prison, and if anything, the prison promoted and displayed the very same behaviors that got these men into prison in the first place. This is a huge problem that we have, not only in U.S. prisons but in prisons all over the world. Exploitation runs rampant in prison, and statistics show that people usually end up going back to prison after a certain amount of time. The general idea of prison is that the inmate will learn his/her lesson through limited exposure to freedom of any type and not want to go back, therefore not committing another crime that will put them right back into the same situation.

The problem is that many people keep going back to institutions and have been since childhood. It ends up being a place of comfort for them instead of a place of punishment because they have had no way of learning any other way. How do we expect human being to learn their lesson and change for the better and be productive members of society when the same corruption outside the penitentiary occurs inside?

It is no surprise that prison is supposed to be a place of punishment, where an individual is sent away to pay for their wrongdoings and reflect on their behavior and the harm that it caused others. Many people have this idea that they should rot in jail for the pain they have caused others and that they deserve this type of treatment. It is agreeable to a certain extent, but on the other hand, it is useful to think about what causes these individuals to lead a life of crime in the first place and what could be done to help these people become better while locked up.

Often times the same behavior that got these men and women into prison in the first place is continued while incarcerated. This is partly due to the fact that prison is better at punishing people rather than helping to rehabilitate them. Wouldn't it make more sense to have certain classes and programs implemented in our prison systems so that these men and women can at least have some sort of a chance of bettering their lives and the lives of others?

Prisoners would have a much better chance at exiting prison and honest and all-around better human beings if rehabilitation were one of the top concerns instead of pure punishment. "Participating in art projects can be particularly helpful in building social networks and providing contexts in which new identities can be embedded, nurtured, and sustained. This is especially true of those interventions that involve public performances that have both internal (e.g., prison officers) and external (e.g., family) audiences because they recognize and celebrate prisoners' achievements and hence encourage positive self-images" In Donovan State Prison, I did not come across much rehabilitation at all.

I remember thinking while working in the prison and watching the inmates that these men seemed to be living the same way inside as they did outside. They had little to no option for recovery. Their bad behavior was met with more bad behavior from the guards, and this just caused the cycle to continue. Rehabilitation, I do not even know what that word means, at least as far as prisons and corrections go.

Most criminals find themselves in a vicious cycle of violence, theft, and perjury that was learned very young. People are products of their environment, and it is very difficult to break the cycle, so to speak. Addiction to alcohol and drugs may also play a large part in these crimes being committed and sometimes get even worse when incarcerated because it helps the time pass and makes it easier to be living under such harsh circumstances, even behind prison walls.

People forget that prisoners are human, too, with real thoughts and feelings. They have more difficulty expressing emotions, which often come out in violent and aggressive ways. This is why it is so important to implement programs in prison so that these men/women actually have a chance at being productive members of society and contributing to life rather than taking from it. "Bureau of Justice Statistics studies have found high recidivism rates among released prisoners. One study tracked 404,638 prisoners in 30 states after their release from prison in 2005.[1] The researchers found that within three years of release, about two-thirds (67.8 percent) of released prisoners were rearrested, and within five years of release, about three-quarters (76.6 percent) of released prisoners were rearrested".

Although prison life should be anything but comfortable and cozy, the United States contains some of the worst prisons in the entire world, using solitary confinement as one of its top torture tactics. Researchers have found that the practice of solitary confinement on an individual leads to damaging and sometimes lifelong threats to one's emotional and mental well-being.

"Researchers have demonstrated that prolonged solitary confinement causes a persistent and heightened state of anxiety and nervousness, headaches, insomnia, lethargy or chronic tiredness, nightmares, heart palpitations, and fear of impending nervous breakdowns. Other documented effects include obsessive ruminations, confused thought processes, an oversensitivity to stimuli, irrational anger, social withdrawal, hallucinations, violent fantasies, emotional flatness, mood swings, chronic depression, feelings of overall deterioration, as well as suicidal ideation."

Even after short periods of confinement, prisoners still show signs of the negative effects solitary confinement has on a human being. They tend to not only be difficult to stimulate but frequently become extremely violent, suicidal, and unable to be rehabilitated after the fact. John is a perfect example of the wear and tear of prison life on a human being. John seemed like a reasonably nice fellow. When it was time for John to be released, he was terrified. On the inside, John felt like someone who was important. There is no doubt that it is extremely difficult to recondition a person after years of living life a certain way. I think that establishing programs for these men and women emphasizing the importance of education would benefit not only the individual serving time but our entire nation.

Some may think that "once a criminal, always a criminal," and these people will never be able to change who they are and how they operate in life. I firmly believe that people can change if they want to. I have seen it happen. It would make a good amount of sense if prisoners were treated and housed in a way that would represent what they should behave like when they are finally released from the institution. How are they to know any different, learn different actions, and take on a positive role in society, being stuck in a room all day long with nothing productive to do or think about?

For many, the time spent behind bars will push them farther into a life of crime, but for others, the horrors of prison life and the lessons they learn there are enough to deter them from committing crimes again in the future." This got me thinking about our society and how we view those that have chosen (or indirectly chosen) to go down the wrong path. After researching prison and rehabilitation in such great depth, I have been really trying to understand prisoners on a deeper level. As a society, we should be concerned with the way our prison system is set up.

Although there are some prisons in the United States that offer some rehabilitation programs to their prisoners, there are so many out there that are completely isolated from any education and personal and moral improvement. Correctional programs are incredibly important in correcting bad behavior, and making sure that these men and women get the help they need while in there would be extremely beneficial to everyone in society.

I believe that programs such as counseling, mental health, fitness, prayer, meditation, and educational programs will help these people see that they do, in fact, have something to contribute to society instead of committing crimes and using violence as a way to get what they want and need in life. They are so much more than that; most have never been told otherwise. The crime life is a vicious cycle, and so is the aggressive and destructive behavior that typically comes along with it, so what good is it to continue checking bad behavior with sometimes even worse behavior? It is not working, and if the general public can rally together, we can make a change and bring the rate of recidivism down.

The Main Goal of the Prison System

The main goal of prison systems needs to be the rehabilitation of prisoners and their reintroduction into the world. We only need to keep the hazardous ones to society or serve a life sentence locked up to keep others safe. All prisons must work under strict orders on what they can and cannot do. We need people to be turned around and benefit society. The putative benefits of more incarceration or longer sentences are costs (Furman 1). There need to be prisons for holding people for the rest of their lives and prisons to help rehabilitate people to join the world who realize that they made a mistake and need a second chance in life. We can no longer function with this single prison system; there is just too vast of a selection of people for the prison to only have one option.

Currently, the prison's primary goal is to take people who commit a crime and put them in time, only to be re-released to commit the same crime. Prisons are meant to be a place for people to be rehabilitated, but it seems it only promotes illegal activity and the membership of gangs. This causes a lot of good people who could make a positive change in their lives to turn for the worse and commit more crimes after they are released.

U.S. prisons should be governed by a national system, which would include all jails and rehabilitation facilities for those who are rehabilitating and intending to return to society positively. There also needs to be a system where prisoners can report complaints to an association for prisoners' rights to make sure they are still being treated the way they deserve to be.

In the prisons, the people who are unable to reintegrate into society, such as murderers and serial killers, need to pay for what they have done to society, but they do not need to suffer. They need to have access to exercise, religious activities, and reading; if they want to get closer to God, it could help them spiritually, even though they have no chance of getting out of prison. They should also be allowed to work to make money to buy things like tobacco products; their work should benefit society, Such as cleaning up roads and making things the state sells, such as license plates.

They need to have a minimum number of hours to work a week but can work more if they choose to. They need to have around an hour a day of rec time where they can exercise and talk with others. If they do something to get in trouble, depending on the act they committed, they should lose all rec time and be locked up in solitary confinement depending on the act they committed.

Those who will be locked up for the rest of their lives do not need to go through any torture. The only punishment they should have to go through is being locked up, and if they commit a terrible act on the inside, solitary confinement. The only prisoners that need to be punished in the U.S.A. are terrorists or people who know something that could save the lives of Americans.

There should be an organization that must train all of the guards on how they are expected to run the jail, with updates occurring every few months, to guarantee that all inmates receive the same level of care. Because they constitute "cruel and unusual" punishment, inhumane circumstances in prisons violate the Eighth Amendment's provision that inmates have the right to be free from "cruel and unusual" punishment. Even if they are in prison for committing heinous crimes, they are still humans and are entitled to some rights.

The other prison system we need to have is for those who committed less serious crimes and want to have a second chance and to be able to make up for the wrong they did. It should be more of a rehabilitation prison. They should be allowed to have access to a class system where they can learn about any type of career they want to go into after they leave prison. They also should be able to review their record and search for any flaws that may have led to them being wrongly convicted. The fundamental purpose of their incarceration should be to ensure that the prisoner leaves with a positive outlook and the necessary resources to reintegrate into society.

While they are inside the prison, they should be in charge of many of the prison duties. Those who want to be a cook should cook food for the prisoners, and those who want to go into clothing should be in charge of repairing the prisoners' clothing. The majority of their day should either be spent studying or practicing the career they want to go in. They also need to have someone knowledgeable in their career to help them with their studies if they have any questions.

In their free time, they should be allowed to walk around the prison for most of the time and be able to work out, talk, play games, watch TV, or study. Fitness should be a big part of the prisoner's life; it will help them work around some schedule and help improve their body in the meantime. The only way to get in trouble is by breaking a set rule and serving the punishment that goes along with it, and repeat offenders are served a harsher punishment. The time they spend in prison should be almost enjoyable in learning about a career they choose to go into.

There should be absolutely no torture or mistreatment in this prison system. Suppose they are in a detention center rather than jail. In that case, they will learn how to reintegrate back into society and become contributing members of society rather than just inmates hoping to avoid re-incarceration.

For the rehabilitation prisons, there still needs to be some form of deterrence from them going into the prisons, and they need to make up for the wrong that they did to society.

In addition, they need to do jobs for the community, such as cleaning roads, painting public buildings, taking care of public parks, and doing other productive things for society.

They can also go to schools with supervisors and talk to them about what they did to go to prison and help try to teach the kids life lessons to help them later on. If they use their own life experiences to help guide younger people, they are making something positive out of something negative and changing their lives by learning a new skill.

There should also be a stricter service for ex-convicts to talk to once freed and returned to society. Currently, the parole/probation officer program is flawed; too many corrupt people are in the system. It needs to be redone, and the officers need to be under strict rules regarding how they can act towards prisoners outside the prison and are trying to get back into the working world. There should be mandatory drug testing for all people in the parole program, and they should stay in their program until the supervisor sees it fit that they are ready to move into the real world.

The goal of prisons should be to help rehabilitate the ones who made a poor choice and keep dangerous people locked up and out of the real world.

The prison system is looked upon as a part of our society that is needed yet doesn't work. Like Jim Hightower said in 1988, "Do something; if it doesn't work, do something else." Since the rehabilitation process doesn't work, we must do something about it. We must change the rehabilitation process so that it works and released prisoners come out of prison as new men with pride and a feeling that they belong outside the gates. How can the prison system rehabilitate prisoners to enter society as equals?

Prison inmates are some of the most "maladjusted" people in society. Most of the inmates have had too little discipline or too much, come from broken homes, and have no self-esteem. They are very insecure and are "at war with themselves and society." Most inmates did not learn moral values or learn to follow everyday norms. Also, when most lawbreakers are labeled criminals, they enter the phase of secondary deviance. They will admit they are criminals or believe it when they enter the phase of secondary deviance. Most inmates find themselves behind bars or abusing drugs and alcohol within three years of being released.

Some believe that if we want to rehabilitate criminals, we must do more than send them to prison. For instance, we could give them a chance to acquire job skills, which will improve the chances that inmates will become productive citizens upon release. The programs must aim to change those who want to change. In the case of Jean Sanders, it was seen that it is hard to stay off drugs and away from the lifestyle you lead. "Like most who leave prison, he will be returning to the scene of his crimes." Those who are taught to produce valuable goods and be productive are "likely to develop the self-esteem essential to a normal, integrated personality."

This program would provide skills and habits and "replace the sense of hopelessness" that many inmates have. Moreover, another technique used to rehabilitate criminals is counseling. There are two types of counseling in general, individual and group counseling. Individual counseling is much more costly than group counseling. Group counseling aims to develop positive peer pressure that will influence its members.

One idea in many sociology texts is that group problem-solving has definite advantages over individual problem-solving. The idea is that a wider variety of solutions can be derived by drawing from the experience of several people with different backgrounds. Also, another group member might have already solved one individual's problem and can be suggested. Often if a peer proposes a solution, it carries more weight than if the counselor suggests it.

Further, in sociology, one of the significant theories of delinquency is differential association. This means some people learned their ways from "undesirable" people they were forced to be in association with and that this association "warps" their thinking and social attitudes. "Group counseling, group interaction, and other kinds of group activities can provide a corrective, positive experience that might help to offset the earlier delinquent association." However, it is said that group counseling can do little to destroy the power of labeling. The differential-association theory emphasizes that a person is more likely to become a criminal if they have the most significant influence upon them are criminals.

Most of today's correctional institutions lack the ability and programs to rehabilitate the criminals of America. One can predict that a prisoner held for two, four, eight, or ten years, then released, still with no education or vocational skills, will likely return to a life of crime. Often their life in crime will resume weeks after their release. Although the best prisons and programs in the world will not completely cure the problem, improvements must be made. Also, being released from prison gives former inmates a disadvantage compared to others. For instance, members of the group might not be as open or show emotion because they want to appear "tough." Also, the members might not express their opinions openly because others might see it as "snitching." It takes a dedicated counselor for the group to work

Some believe that a way to stop crime is to punish criminals much more. This was contradicted by what Mr. Resko stated. "Punishment did nothing for the felon except make him warier, more cunning, and more inclined to violence. Punishment was not the answer to the financial and moral problems generated by the increasing number of prisons and prisoners. Whether corporal, psychological, or moral, punishment is not the answer. Not for the con or for his respectable brother."

Another type of correctional center used for rehabilitation is a halfway house. Halfway houses are usually located in residential communities and aim to keep offenders in the community. The name comes from the fact that they are "halfway between the community and the prison." The "rationale" behind halfway houses is that criminal activity originates in the community, so the community has a responsibility to correct it. Also, sending a person who has deviant behavior associated with criminal influences to prison would worsen the problem. "The best place for treatment is in the community; this prevents breaking all constructive social ties" To experiment on this hypothesis, we must do a longitudinal study. Inmates must be studied from the time they enter the prison system until approximately 5 or 10 years after being released. A survey must be given to find suitable candidates, and those who are as similar to each other as possible will be the people studied. Questions about the background (religion, manners, schooling, first time committing a crime, etc.), crime committed, age, sex, sexual preference, and hobbies will be asked on the questionnaire to identify similarities and differences.

The background is essential because it made this person who he is today. Also, it is what identifies a person most. The crime committed should be the same one so that we do not see the progress of murderers compared to people that committed a white-collar crime. Age is relevant because the younger we are, the more easily influenced we are. Sex is essential because we must study one group and sexual preference. After all, the difference in appearance, as well as lifestyle, is easily seen. Hobbies are a significant factor because it is said that a person that has hobbies can overcome an ordeal easier than a person without.

In my study, there are a lot of influences; however, they cannot be altered since they are part of life. The dependent variable is the outcome of a person after being released from prison once completing a new rehabilitation program. The independent variables are such things as peers that surround the person, the toughness of the guards, and the amount spent in the new rehabilitation program. Each independent variable can cause the dependent variable to have a different outcome. There will be many trials to see the appropriate way to achieve the most advantageous to society method. In the end, the question is, how can the prison system rehabilitate prisoners so that they will enter society as equals?

I believe this study is that prisoners who get educated will have an easier transition than prisoners who were not educated and were still rehabilitated the same way the prison system now works. An educated inmate will be able to integrate into society as if they were at home, yet, a prisoner who was not educated or kept up to date will have a more difficult time and be perceived as inferior to those not in prison. The world is still based on survival of the fittest, and one must have a brain and brawn to survive and even be identified. Prisoners with the same level of intelligence as they were when they entered the prison system will have a significant disadvantage over those who have been schooled and shaped. However, those who were schooled while in prison will have a slight disadvantage only because they have a record.

In conclusion, things need to be done to improve rehabilitation in America. Improvements in job training, counseling, and halfway houses for rehabilitation must be brought to the forefront by citizens. If we do not get involved and try to make changes, our crime problem could worsen beyond our control. This is essential to study since the Bureau of Justice Statistics states that we have more than 1 million prisoners in the United States, and the number is climbing daily. As a result of the fact that most formerly incarcerated individuals re-offend shortly after being released and return to prison within three years, those who are freed do not belong in society. We must educate them to have a regular job and an everyday life, one that stays away from prison and away from breaking the law when released.

Return to Society from Prison

Parole and reentry are two terms from different ends of the spectrum when describing how prisoners find themselves back in their respective communities after serving a prison sentence. Reentry is a strategy in which offenders are prepared to return home from prison, and parole is simply a matter of supervision.

According to Gideon and Sung, a person who has been released from prison but is still subject to the authorities' surveillance is said to be on parole. In general, parole was designed initially as a crime reduction strategy intended to ensure the community's safety. However, parole has not seemed to reduce the number of offenders who continue to recycle through the criminal justice system.

Parole involves several conditions assigned to the offender to hold the offender accountable for his actions in the community. As part of these required conditions, the offender is subjected to a predetermined level of monitoring based on the level of risk he poses to the community's safety. The focal point of the monitoring function is compliance and external control by the correctional institutions that place such demands on offenders. The responsibility of meeting the assigned monitoring condition is solely on the offender, and the process is relentlessly unforgiving.

Under the conditions of parole supervision, the offender is responsible for paying his supervision costs even if he is unemployed or cannot afford basic life necessities. Additionally, the offender is expected to find and attend treatment even if it is not locally available in the community; he is responsible for staying sober and living in a sober environment. He is to find employment and comply with any other conditions placed upon him by the controlling authorities of the parole office.

The parolee under supervision has an increased potential to violate the terms of his release due to the increasing number of supervision requirements. The unintended consequences of violations might result in an offender returning to Prison. Added curfew conditions, drug testing, house arrest, or even electronic monitoring provide several ways for an offender to become non-compliant and fail to meet expectations.

Many parole officers have taken a law enforcement perspective and strictly enforced the conditions of release. This has succeeded only in creating a bitter relationship between the officer and the offender. By emphasizing responsibility and accountability, parole agencies have developed a solely punitive character. It has been shown that increasing the intensity of supervision has done nothing to improve the outcomes for offenders. It is an unfortunate reality that there are funds to provide tools for monitoring an offender in the world of parole. However, few dollars are spent on behavioral interventions that help parolees learn to change their thinking patterns and ways of life.

Reentry

Reentry is simply the process of leaving prison and returning to society. It is not a form of supervision like parole. Prisoner reentry includes all the programs and activities involved in assisting former inmates to become productive members of society as they integrate into their communities. Preparing inmates for release rarely concerns prison officials. Most inmates are released from prison with little regard for rehabilitation or reentry. This is a disastrous practice, as prisoner reentry is not an optional strategy. Reentry is "an unavoidable result of incarceration because virtually all inmates will be released from prison." The incarceration binge that occurred in the 80s and 90s resulted in a massive increase in the prisoner population. Nearly 95% will be released after serving a year behind bars. These offenders will return to their communities with significant disadvantages.

Challenges to Reentry

There are many barriers to reentry. The convicted felon is denied the right to vote; they are not granted access to student loans, welfare benefits, public housing, or food stamps. In addition, these released offenders regularly return to communities experiencing social decay, are plagued by poverty, and have few employment opportunities. They are also denied entry into several employment fields due to their status as a felon. Denying them assistance and a social safety net often hinders their reentry abilities and transformation into law-abiding citizens. As mentioned prior, the added burden of intensive supervision can also be problematic for successful reentry.

Effective Reentry Programs

Prisoners who have extensive criminal histories, abuse drugs and or alcohol, and are unemployed are more likely to re-offend and have reentry problems. With that in mind, a successful reentry program should target for change those who are considered high risk, should involve an element of a therapeutic community, and include some cognitive-behavioral programs.

The therapeutic community (T.C.) is an extremely structured program isolated from the rest of the prison. This community is structured for those considered high-risk offenders and drug offenders. T.C. s are considered highly effective because they separate high-risk offenders from the violence and drug use associated with prison life.

Within the T.C., staff members and inmates hold each other accountable for their actions using an aggressive communication style. The focus of treatment is on the underlying disorders and psychological problems and not the drug use." The result of this type of treatment is that residents learn to be accountable for their actions and function as members of a community. Both skills, along with drug treatment, are beneficial for effective reentry.

Cognitive-behavioral therapy (C.B.T.) programs are founded on the idea that cognitive habits determine human emotions and behaviors like beliefs and thoughts. If the prominent elements of criminal thinking, such as entitlement, power, control, over-optimism, and self-justification, can be addressed, the offender can learn pro-social cognitive habits.

The C.B.T. focuses on teaching offenders personal responsibility and helps them understand the thinking patterns and decisions that occur before their anti-social activities. Positive changes begin to occur when offenders start to self-monitor and modify their problematic criminal thinking, resulting in positive attitudes and healthy reasoning skills.

In addition to T.C. and C.B.T. programs, other elements of effective reentry should include the offender participating in basic educational programs, which increase their employment potential and may bolster their confidence.

With that, an effective vocational program that teaches the offender a marketable job skill in a field not limited to him by having a felony status would address the unemployment issue and provide a stable foundation upon reentry. Finally, teaching the offender essential money management and budgeting skills can provide him with the necessary means of addressing everyday situations and eliminating some of the stress.

With these incarceration-based programs, T.C., C.B.T., education, vocation, and money management should also be added to aftercare programs that help the offender continue to practice the pro-social skills they have learned. In addition, an aftercare program has the potential to provide the offender with a cohort of sorts who can help him understand his struggles because they, too, are experiencing the same situations. The aftercare program also provides the offender with access to resources and community connections to aid the reentry process.

To summarize, parole and reentry encompass two very different philosophies, the former being one of supervision and the latter being the process by which one returns to society. However, they do both affect an offender's success or failure upon returning to the community. They can also work together to help an offender succeed. With the proper incarceration-based programming, effective aftercare treatment, and a parole agent focused on helping the offender succeed (as opposed to enforcement), a former inmate will have increased chances of improving his outcomes in life and avoiding re-incarceration.

Sentencing in the United States represents what to do about crime and the criminal offender. The choice of sentencing is punishment, which serves copious social control functions while imposing consequences for one's criminal actions. Punishment is generally justified by retribution, incapacitation, deterrence, rehabilitation, and restoration, and sentencing strategies vary among the different philosophies.

Rehabilitation

In rehabilitation, the goal is to change the factors that cause an offender to break the law. The assumption is that crime is determined by anti-social attitudes, anti-social peers, and dysfunctional families. Criminal behavior will continue without addressing and targeting these criminogenic needs for change.

Sentencing Policies of Rehabilitation

The rehabilitation philosophy involves policies including indeterminate sentences. The court sets a minimum prison term an offender must serve before becoming eligible for parole. This provides judges with significant discretion to tailor the punishment to the offender. Furthermore, parole is considered a critical correctional policy of rehabilitation (Cullen & Jonson, 2012, p. 14). The parole board is also granted vast discretion to retain offenders for continued treatment or release them. Treatment programs are included both in prison and after release.

The System is Broken

The 13th Amendment to the American Constitution is celebrated and known as the amendment to end slavery. The amendment states, "Neither slavery nor involuntary servitude, except a punishment for crime whereof the party shall have been duly convicted, shall exist within the United States, or any place subject to their jurisdiction" (U.S. Constitution, Amendment 13). What is often overlooked is that this amendment abolishes slavery unless you are a criminal. After the Civil War, this loophole was wildly used by slave owners, as they would convict African Americans of minor crimes to then use them as slaves again. This exception to the amendment is continually used today in the American prison system.

The Criminal Justice System in America contains significant flaws that are detrimental to society. A few of these flaws lie within the actions and ideals of the prison system, the policies and laws surrounding the criminal justice system, and the American Legislative Exchange Council.

The reality of the conditions in American prisons is that a majority of Americans would not even keep their pets in the same environment that prisoners are kept in. In addition, a majority of prison guards are only required to have a high school diploma. The low standards for prison guards create a breeding ground for a lack of empathy, a presence of sexual assault, and an abuse of power. Anyone who has been to prison would confidently say that it is not a fun place to be. A favored rebuttal to the existence of these conditions is that the population of people in prisons are criminals and that they should be punished. However, it is often noted that the prison system in America is designed to break a person down in thirty days, and many prisoners suffer from the negative psychological impacts of incarceration. These conditions do not at all help to rehabilitate prisoners back into society, thus causing a recidivism rate of nearly two-thirds (Prison Policy Initiative). Similarly to the conditions of the prisons, the laws and policies surrounding them are equally as unjust and unfair. A few examples of these are mandatory minimums, plea bargains, the price of bail, and lost rights. Mandatory minimums, which came into effect under the Clinton administration, declare minimum sentencing times for certain state and federal crimes. These sentencing laws prevent judges from forming a sentence based on the individual and the circumstances present.

Mandatory minimum sentencing laws are only prevalent in nineteen of the fifty states, but they significantly increased prison populations, overcrowding, and taxpayer costs nonetheless (Families Against Mandatory Minimums). Plea bargaining is commonly used to save time and money, seeing as a trial does not have to take place. Around ninety percent of criminal cases result in plea bargains, meaning those people never made it in front of a judge and jury. Many defendants accept these plea bargains to reduce their harsh mandated prison sentences, even if they are innocent. Oftentimes, defendants are pressured to accept these bargains because the idea of going to trial and gambling their odds of freedom or long prison time is scary (PBS).

The question of equity remains about these bargains, considering everyone has a constitutional right to a fair trial. Plea bargains are rooted heavily in inconvenience, and the unfairness of these bargains is heavily tied to mandatory minimums.

Another issue is the bail system, which allows defendants to await their trial at home rather than in jail for a set price. The idea is that the defendant will pay the money and promise to return for trial, where they will be given back their money. However, the bail system is unfair to lower-class people who cannot afford the set bail price. In turn, those people awaiting trial who are "innocent until proven guilty" are stuck in jail. As Michelle Alexander said, "There are thousands of people in jails right this moment that are sitting there for no other reason than because they're too poor to get out." This consequentially wastes the slim amount of resources in prisons and uses up taxpayer dollars (13th).

After a person exits prison, their criminal record, which is extremely difficult to expunge, follows them around forever. Certain rights guaranteed to all Americans are lost when you have been convicted of a crime. Once you have a criminal record, you cannot vote, own guns, apply for public social benefits, or work for a public agency. It is also difficult to travel abroad and find jobs that hire former convicts (The Law Dictionary). The American Legislative Exchange Council (ALEC) is at the root of corruption in America's criminal justice system. ALEC is a nonprofit organization that brings together politicians and big corporations. Through ALEC, corporate lobbyists and lawmakers come together to secretly vote on bills that are then introduced to become laws in the states. In turn, laws that are created by ALEC eventually generate profit for one of the ALEC corporations, while the politicians take credit for the laws they proposed as their own.

The problem with ALEC is derived from the power that major corporations have over America's laws. The Stand, Your Ground law enacted in Florida generated a huge increase in gun sales, presumably benefiting Walmart, the biggest seller of guns in America and a longtime member of ALEC (13th Documentary). The population of ALEC members also includes a variety of corporations that profit off of inmates, such as Aramark, which provides food in prison, and the Corrections Corporation of America (CCA), which maintains the prisons. Laws proposed by ALEC, such as Mandatory Minimum Sentencing and Third Strike laws, consequentially increased the inmate population in America and thus increased profit for these corporations.

The "nonprofit" organization ALEC creates a dangerous connection between lawmakers and major corporations and treats the incarcerated unfairly. Positive changes to the criminal justice system must begin with awareness, as corruption in the system is often overlooked. These changes will not be possible unless the people and politicians recognize its destruction. However, once these positive changes are implemented, unprecedented prosperity will occur not only in the criminal justice system but in all of

America as well.

Today our criminal justice system has a large number of alternatives when managing the individuals who are indicted on offenses; fines, probation, group administration, transient sentences in prison, or more sentences in an assortment of diverse-level jails, and a definitive discipline is still passing. Our objectives are clear and direct, stop the conduct, make compensation, educate new abilities, and for some, restore through treatment, medication, and/or alcohol and drug counseling. Shockingly, there are those that are esteemed, unredeemable, and unfit to ever come back to society, and they are either bound in jail until their common passing or sentenced to bite the dust by the request of the state or government. Barring capital punishment, being given a sentence to jail is our harshest discipline. Because of congestion, the "group," and the absence of individual control, it's a perilous spot to be in. A sexual and physical strike is normal, seclusion is a mental test, and the general environment is a passionate bad dream.

There are seven objectives of sentencing, including restoration, just deserts, retribution, incapacitation, deterrence, rehabilitation, and revenge.

Revenge alludes to a striking back to some ambush and harm. Vengeance can be a sort of discipline for the criminal justice system. The jury, once in a while, constructs their decisions with respect to feelings, certainties, and confirmation. It is considered revenge now and again in light of the fact that the casualty takes a gander at it that way when they feel equity has been served.

Retribution is a sort of sentencing, including another type of countering. Retribution signifies "paying back" the wrongdoer for what he or she has done. The victim is not the only one with regard to being influenced by the wrongdoing. Society is emphatically influenced by what a criminal does in whichever territory he or she picks Throughout time, a theory known as the deterrence effect has been proposed to society as capital punishment. People assume that if you achieve something incorrectly, for this circumstance, you kill a person, then you will be executed theory keeping you from presenting that wrong action again. This theory furthermore communicates that by auditing or getting some answers concerning your order, others around you won't copy your illustration, reducing the number of criminal acts executed. Although revenge may make you feel better about the situation, it is not Justice. "With God as my witness, I have been deceitfully accused of these wrongdoings. I did not commit them. I am a guiltless man, and I just pray in the name of Jesus Christ that all this will be brought out. The truth will ultimately be carried out." Calvin C. Johnson Jr. stated this in 1983, at his sentence hearing

Penitentiaries and correctional facilities are both considered incapacitation. Prison is where individuals lack personal freedom and are physically restricted from daily activities they are used to in the free world. Furthermore, those anticipating trials and those serving a term surpassing one year are limited here, while a correctional facility or jail is the place detainees are housed preceding their trials on the nearby level and those serving a term of one year or less.

Utilizing discipline to restore a criminal is similar to utilizing an ice pack to try and fix a broken arm. Every remedy only attempts to amend just the side effects or symptoms, yet once they are taken away, the issue is still there. As a weed must be removed by its roots, the crime must be wiped out by decimating its basic underlying causes. The bases of wrongdoing are frequently a consequence of a man's estrangement from society, which takes his poise and worth. Subsequently, this causes sentiments of separation and powerlessness and wrecks any sentiment of moral obligation to that community. At the end of the day, he will have no individual enthusiasm for nor the ability to impact his group, and in this way, he can't think about its destiny. As a consequence of his indifference, he will have little protest to putting his own welfare over that of the community by violating the law. A criminal with the right to rehabilitation can be transformed from a threat to society into one of its most significant resources.

Another method used to restore inmates is counseling. There are two sorts of counseling when all is done: individual and group advising. Individual counseling is significantly more immoderate than group advising. The point of group advising is to create a positive associate weight that will impact its individuals. One thought is that group problem-solving and critical thinking have unequivocal preferences over individual critical thinking or counseling. The thought is that a more extensive assortment of solutions can be derived by drawing from the experience of a few individuals with diverse foundations. Likewise, one person's issue may have been solved by another member of the group and can be recommended. Regularly if another member of the group were to propose an answer, it would convey more weight than if the counselor were to recommend it.

To manage wrongdoing, we should first go to the base of the issue. The American culture is a reproducing ground for violent crime. Protection measures must be executed to stop such conduct before it begins. Showing family values in after-school projects is a stage in the right course. Programs that show admiration teach respect, responsibility, and anger management for one's own behavior is an unquestionable requirement in today's general public.

Jail programs for first-time inmates offering some assistance with becoming productive, law-abiding citizens of society can be a stage in the right bearing. Showing inmates how to oversee anger, medication and alcohol counseling, relationship-building activities, and in addition showing hands-on skills to prisoners will facilitate the move from jail to the outside world (Cullen.) At the point when the prisoner is discharged, a shelter ought to be the home of the previous detainee until changes are made. Along these lines, a man coming into society won't be overpowered by his freshly discovered opportunity. Giving them back a piece of their freedom, one day at a time.

Cognitive Behavior Treatment

The traditional method to reintegrate an offender into the general population requires constant direct supervision of the offender and their environment. Behavioral psychologists have spent time and effort researching how social learning connects to socially acceptable behavior. Many offenders in the system were arrested and placed due to not knowing the correct way to behave and act in the general population. Depending on the offender's past or current lifestyle, it may not be acceptable for them to act according to how one should act due to how peers look at the offender or how the environment influences them.

Often the behavioral thinking patterns are set deep enough so that it would take severe re-conditioning to change. Old patterns have to be destroyed, and new behaviors reinforced adequately.

The elements that support the environment in which social learning can occur are structure and accountability. Learning structure allows the offender to move toward a common goal of the proper way to live in modern society. Psychologists and counselors work with offenders to provide a rehabilitating learning environment in which "values, rules, roles, and responsibilities" are the base. The offender shifts from an observer stance, vehemently denying and resisting authority, to a participant stance. They are willing to comply but are still mentally operating in a criminal mode, and finally, to a properly functioning society member stance. Accountability teaches respect for structure and moves the offender through these stages (a willing participant who shares the new values of good living in a decent society). The environment also provides the opportunity for practice and success.

Eventually, as the offender is working their way through the entire process, they will continually be reinforced with positive benefits and hopefully build self-efficacy. This is where cognitive behavior therapy plays a significant role in improving offenders' lifestyles.

Cognitive behavior therapy programs operate with some common assumptions. Problematic behavior is primarily rooted in the ways of thinking that promote and support such behavior. For example, please look at a person who has stolen property all his life. Due to that offender's corrupted thought process, he believes that the only way to obtain property is to take it with no one knowing or by force without regard to consequences. To change this problematic behavior, one must change their beliefs and attitudes and modify the way of thinking. Punitive methods of controlling behavior reinforce modes of thinking that we're responsible for the initial anti-social behavior.

Authority helps to pinpoint rules and assists in reinforcing consequences while reminding and encouraging offenders to make their own decisions. As offenders learn to make conscious and deliberate life choices, they take responsibility for their behavior. The programs that offenders go through to change their thought processes can also teach pro-social behavior. Even severe or high-risk criminals can change their thinking patterns and become more socially acceptable. The values that are taught in any cognitive program can also be applied in many other ways.

These ways include such categories as victim restitution, education, and personal development.

There are two main types of approaches to cognitive programs. They are cognitive skills and reconstructing. This method of retraining criminals in social skills such as conflict resolution, negotiation, anger management, and others is founded on the premise that they have never developed the necessary cognitive thinking skills to function correctly and responsibly in society.

Restructuring is based on the idea that offenders have learned destructive attitudes and habits that lead to criminal behavior. Restructuring involves locating and isolating the attitudes and ways of thinking that create criminal behavior. Both restructuring and skill-based methods can be used in any single program to teach an offender and accelerate the process.

John's Story

I was raised in a family where there was an authoritarian and an enabler as parents. Consequently, I lived in fear daily and sympathy at the same time. My Stepmother was the only person I knew who did not use drugs or alcohol or inappropriate behavior. I tried to tell myself that I would never be like my dad, but I would turn out just like him, if not worst. By the time I was thirteen, I was drinking alcohol, smoking cigarettes, taking pills, smoking weed, and doing time as a juvenile.

I left home around this time and had to learn how to survive independently. This went on until I was 21 years old and ended up in prison; I got married and had a child just before I went to prison. I had this reputation for violence, so my wife at the time asked me for divorce just before I was released.

That was in the Sixties, and I got out in the seventies. I do not know how many times I went to prison. I just know I had two numbers, a "B" number and a "C" number. I went a few times on the C number. Every time I went to prison, I continued to work on my survival skills. At least that's what we called them, but we were just looking for the easier, softer way to beat the system while making enough money to survive.

My first experience in prison was filled with fear initially, but as time went on, I started to get used to all the riots, threats of violence, and watching my back. I finally accepted the fact that rehabilitation was a joke. Suppose anyone was going to get anything that resembled rehabilitation.

In that case, he would have to get it on his own by reading, writing, and sharing his experiences with other people trying to change themselves.

Prison life is hard, and the psychological effects are far-reaching. They touch every part of your life. If you don't build up a hard-core image, somebody will try to take you down, and from that point on, every day, you will live or die trying to protect that image, so much so that you take it home with you and live the same way on the streets. This picture became so crucial in my life that I grew to rely on it for everything.

I did not become aware of my image's effects on me until I decided to change my life. I went into a drug and alcohol treatment program in 1993, and it was in that program I learned how my image was affecting my life. I had been going to jail, going to prison, and using drugs for many years before someone helped me see my real problem, and believe it or not, it was my image driving me like a wild animal. I finally realized that it was my image that I loved doing drugs. I loved doing time, the fast life, violence, lying, cheating, and manipulating people out of their money so I could feed the habits I had developed over the years. Once I let go of this image, the things I mentioned went with it. That's when I found out that I had just uncovered the first layer of this image. Now I had to replace all that negativity with something positive; I learned to live a normal and more respectful lifestyle.

I have been clean from drugs and alcohol for twenty-nine years. I have also been clean from damaging behavior. But I have many issues to work on, like trust, communication, relationships, and being a good husband, father, and friend. As far as my social skills are concerned, I went back to school, became a drug and alcohol counselor, and worked in recovery for over twenty years. Being raised like I was and going to prison so much, I acted like a convict when I got out. I trusted no one; I am a loner, I didn't make friends easily, and I still have a problem with my communication skills, so being locked up in a convict's mind is a serious issue. Let me give you a couple of examples: speaking to my relationships. You just could not let yourself get that close to another man without being in prison and without someone thinking you were funny. So, when I got out, I did not look for things like intimacy, closeness, or romance. In prison, you didn't go around making friends. You road with the San Diego car, which you did when you got out. We had the language that we used with each other, and it had nothing to do with being friendly or respectful to males or females. So, you can see that I did not have any need to learn communication skills. I have missed out on much healthy living because of my lack of living skills or education in areas like love, intimacy, and showing care and concern for those I say you love. Although I am familiar with all these issues, I have a problem putting them into action.

I am not sure why it's so hard for me to put these things into action, but I think the point I am trying to make here is how long it took me to recognize that these things were hurting my marriage and my relationship with everything and everybody in my life. Sometimes I just want to go somewhere, sit down, and start crying because these things make me feel like a failure, and feeling like a failure does not feel good. I mentioned trust. Trust is one of those things a person must earn, and dealing with the type of people I was raised with; it was almost impossible to trust any of them in prison or out. It did not matter.

I spoke about communication skills; well, in the period I was raised in, we did not do much talking; we settled almost everything with a violent confrontation, and it did not matter if it was male or female. We either bought what we wanted, traded for it, or took it. Everything seemed to be done in a hurry. So as far as communication skills are concerned, I did not get involved with these skills until I got into recovery.

As far as relationships are concerned, I have had a tough time with them, whether they were intimate or platonic. I just never found the time to get involved like that; believe it or not, I thought. I understood both when I did not have a clue. The only problem with this was I had to act like I was the lover of all time or the best friend you would ever need. I cannot believe I am writing all this stuff down for anyone to read. I guess it's about time because I have shared it with my sponsor anyway, and this is just my Higher Powers' way of making sure I am being frank. Now that I have given it more thought, I can see why criminals have difficulty letting go of their old ways and starting their lives. That's precisely what I had to do to get where I am today.

Even though I have been working on myself for several years, I have only touched the surface of what I need to understand about growing up and becoming a man. It was tough to accept that I wasn't a real man. I need to say this: being a real man and thinking you're a real man are two completely different things. When it comes to his wife (if he is married), his children (if any), and friends, a real man knows and understands that each of these persons has specific needs, and a man must be able to treat each of these individuals as if they were his own. One of the most challenging issues to deal with is family issues, especially if a man has lived most of his life on the streets and become an addict.

Well, I hope this little insert will help the reader understand what being locked up in the mind of a convict looks like and what they have to go through to re-establish themselves as acceptable, responsible, and productive members of society.

The Development of a Criminal Mind

In today's society, one will find that many different factors go into the development of a criminal mind, and it is impossible to single out one particular cause of criminal behavior. Criminal behavior often stems from both biological and environmental factors. In many cases, criminals share similar physical traits which the general population does not usually have. For example, criminals have smaller brains than adequately adjusted individuals.

However, biological reasons cannot solely be the cause of criminal behavior. Therefore, one must look to other sources of how a criminal mind is developed. Social and environmental factors are also at fault for developing a person to the point where they are led to commit a criminal act.

Often, someone who has committed a violent crime shows evidence of a poorly developed childhood or the unsuitable current conditions in which the subject lives. In addition, if one studies victimology, which is the victim's role in the crime, it is apparent that there are many different causes of criminal behavior. In addition to the social and environmental factors that make up a criminal mind, an examination of biological factors shows that a criminal is often born with traits common to criminals; it is the environment around them that brings out the criminal in them to commit indecent acts of crime.

It is a fact that criminals have smaller brains than law-abiding citizens. Often, offenders share particular physical traits such as being young males, muscular, having lower than average IQ, and having impulsive personalities. Serial offenders are usually hyperactive and challenging children. If a person has a low IQ, it is directly related to their tendency to commit impulse actions that provide an immediate payoff. For instance, a rape or a mugging would provide a criminal with an immediate payoff. It is proven that crime often runs in families. Chronic criminals are three times more likely to have criminal children. However, scientists have no basis to come to any conclusions with this data despite this information. Therefore, one must consider other possible factors that may create a criminal mind, to come to a reasonable decision as to how one is developed.

It is proven that there is a connection between diet and crime. Nutritional deficiency is linked to an increased risk of violent crime. Nutrition can often exacerbate a person's current health issues. Probation officers in Los Angeles have outlawed all pollutants, including chocolate bars and sweets, and refined foods. It was proven that a dietary change to healthy food could lower antisocial behavior by about forty-six percent. Sugar consumption can cause a chain reaction in the body leading to antisocial behavior because the pancreas releases insulin which makes excess glucose. When John Hinckley tried to kill President Regan, he lived on a diet of fast food, coffee, and sugary soft drinks. This shows that our biochemical makeup can also contribute to a person's motivation for criminal behavior. Still, how our body reacts to certain environmental toxins is not a valid explanation for criminal behavior.

In today's society, many factors are proven to provoke acts of violence. Canada's current rate of violent crime is one-fifth of that of the United States, proving that criminal behavior is not solely caused due to hereditary factors. Television contributes significantly to the idea of violence being imprinted onto criminals' minds. If you watch television for one hundred hours, you will witness at least twelve murders. Canada has a much stricter gun control law compared to the USA. If more guns are available, it can be sure that these guns will be used to pursue the crime.

In many cases of violent criminals, we see similar environmental components that exist in the subject's life, which explain the reason for the maladjusted personalities. For instance, a man named Marc LePine committed the unimaginable crime of mass murder of fourteen women, and then he killed himself. But it is pretty evident what could have motivated him to commit this act of insanity.

His father brutally beat LePine as a young boy, and his father imprinted violence on his brain. His father considered women to be the slaves of men. Around the age of two, boys discover they are boys and that their father is also a boy, only a more extensive version; therefore, he is a role model. Marc LePine had a naughty role model and grew up with corrupted morals.

When we are born, our minds are kind of blank. The information we receive in our first five years has a good chance of sustaining itself without being critically evaluated.

As Le Pine got older, his mother left her children with family and relatives and occasionally visited. Losing his mother and father figure was like a double catastrophe for LePine. He focused on this, which led him to live a maladjusted life, eventually killing himself and fourteen girls.

A perfect example of how a person's crime-prone biological factors are often brought out through the environment that they live in, which leads them to commit a crime, is shown through Clifford Boggess. While Boggess's mother was pregnant, she often did drugs, and as Clifford grew up, his personality was described as being a little crazy, and he did not act as ordinary people acted. He craved attention and had a very explosive temper, showing that Clifford had biological factors similar to that of criminals. As Clifford grew up, his mother did drugs, had an alcohol problem, and frequently abused them. He was then adopted, but his adoptive mother abandoned him when she divorced. Clifford felt he had no real connection with his town, and because of these environmental factors and his crime-prone biology, he was led to murder people from his town.

The study of victimology can be used to support the theory that criminals are the product of the society in which they live. This explores the role that the victim plays in the cause of the crime and the notion that there would not be crimes without suitable victims. There are habitual victims, just as there are habitual criminals. There is often an essential interplay between the criminal and their victim. Ninety percent of criminals have some relationship with their victims. The victim is usually chosen for traits that they possess. This suggests that the victim may be partially responsible for the crime of which they were the victim.

Therefore, the criminal's environment and the people around them influence them to commit a criminal act.

In conclusion, examinations show that an average

criminal's biological makeup is often tormented by an unsuitable environment that can lead a person to a crime. Often a criminal possesses biological traits that are fertile soil for criminal behavior. Some people's bodies react irrationally to an abnormal diet, and some are born with criminal traits. But this alone does not explain their motivation for criminal behavior. These people's environment releases the potential for criminal behavior and makes it a reality.

Many environmental factors lead to a person committing a crime, ranging from how they were raised and what kind of role models they followed to having suitable victims almost asking to be victimized. The best way to solve criminal behavior is to find the source of the problem, but this is a very complex issue, and the cause of an act of crime cannot be put on one source.

Made in the USA
Columbia, SC
28 May 2024

36038096R00095